BOOKS BY URSULE MOLINARO

POWER DREAMERS
The Jocasta Complex

A NOVEL BY

Ursule Molinaro

McPherson & Company

POWER DREAMERS

Published by McPherson & Company
Box 1126, Kingston, New York 12401.
Published with assistance from the Literature Programs
of the New York State Council on the Arts and
the National Endowment for the Arts, a federal agency.
Designed by Bruce R. McPherson.
Typeset in Bembo by Studio Graphics.
Manufactured in the United States of America.

Library of Congress Cataloging-in-Publication Data

Molinaro, Ursule.
Power dreamers : the Jocasta complex : a novel / by Ursule Molinaro.
        p.   cm.
    ISBN 0-929701-44-5 : $16.00
              I. Title
      PS3525.O2152P65   1994
    813'.54—dc20   94-37403

First Edition
1 3 5 7 9 10 8 6 4 2
1994 1995 1996 1997 1998 1999

Author's Note

It is my belief that the drastic demotion of women in ancient Greek society occurred in reaction   by the men   to the ritualistic sacrifice of the old king at year's end, (the king symbolized the passage of the seasons; FATHER Time), while the queen (symbolizing MOTHER Nature, or Earth) remained in power until her natural death, annually remarrying a new & young king-consort.

The changeover began with simulating the slaying: The old king was whisked over the city wall, into a waiting boat, or chariot. Still, he remained banished from the city, & condemned to a life of begging. —He was officially dead, & would have to be killed if he was seen.

Eventually the men rebelled by abolishing matrilinear succession, excluding women from their former prerogatives: medicine   magic powers   & religion; leaving them only prophecy, but even there, they became mere mouthpieces for the oracular pronouncements of a male deity (Apollo in Delphi).

The myth of Oedipus, killing his father & marrying his mother, retells the ritualistic slaying of the old king, & the queen's remarriage. The incestuous addition with its tragic retributions for a broken taboo illustrates the initial blasphemy attached to the power shift. Queen Jocasta's suicide is a protest against Oedipus claiming the throne in patrilinear succession. Initially, the erinnies persecute him for causing the death of his mother, the ruling queen, not for killing his father.

CHAPTER 1

Today I finally asked my women if I had lost my looks. They protested in shocked unison: Oh no, Queen Jocasta! & then enumerated all the alleged assets of my face: You are as beautiful as a summer's night. Your hair is like a dark-bluing river of oblivion. Your eyes have the charcoal vigilance of the white owl. Your brows arch like butterfly wings. Your skin has the cool glow of moon beams. & your mouth holds the pink promise of cresting dawn. You are beautiful, Queen Jocasta. As beautiful as the shining moon.

Madame Tiresias said: When the moon distrusted her looks, she quietly slipped behind a cloud. & they all laughed at me.

I was not reassured. Their exaggerated protests sounded like compassion to me. The humiliating compassion for a woman their queen the queen of the 7-gated City of Thebes, with a lion for her emblem whose husband avoids the conjugal couch.

Laius openly proclaims his passion for a young man he brought back with him from Pisa where he spent much of his banishment. A pretty not terribly bright youth appropriately named Chrysippus—the golden horse— whom he is teaching charioteering. He's even talking about setting up a regiment of charioteers, solely composed of men who are lovers, so proud is he of his infatuation. Which he claims to have invented. Proclaiming himself to be the first pederast in the civilized world.

My suggestion   that he picked up the habit from his regular horses, that are known to mount each other when no mare is willing, or from the palace dogs, that will hump anything that feels alive, even a human leg, when the urge comes upon them   started a monologue in which he likened the female sex to a devious abysmal trap, set to catch man's most precious appendage, & drain his strength. Whereas the new form of love   the true form of love/ form of true love   which he invented with Chrysippus doubled the strength of both participants.

I merely shrugged. Chrysippus is 6 years younger than I am, but he treats me as though I were his mother. I was a precocious little girl: I told him: but not precocious enough for motherhood at the age of 6. He gazed at me, his light eyes wide with lack of understanding. Any attempt at humor is wasted, on my husband's idol.

It is any wonder that I have begun to distrust my desirability? Despite my attending women's flowery protest. I've ordered a panel of silver to be polished to highest gloss. I need to see for myself. Checking my reflection in the duck pond blurs what may have become the sharpened contours of my cheeks & chin.

CHAPTER 2

I spent the morning staring into my reflected eyes in the polished silver plate. & I agree with my women, minus their flowery speech: It is not my face, but my husband's boastful infatuation, that prevents him from supplying Thebes with an heir to the throne. A royal duty, that might have been a pleasure, under different circumstances.

Laius & I are distant cousins. Which has never been an obstacle to royal marriages. On the contrary: It consolidates the succession. But now Laius talks to me about the dangers of inbreeding. He fears that our offspring might come out flawed. Perhaps feeble-minded. I think *he* is becoming feeble-minded, in the adulation of his wide-eyed golden boy.

I stared into my eyes until I hypnotized myself. Until images began to appear on the bluish-green screen of my irises. A hippopotamus family, on a grassy terrain in mid-afternoon sunshine. A bull, his dam, & their young son. Who suddenly charged, & killed his astonished sire. Then triumphantly mounted the widowed dam. Who moved her rump obligingly, to guide the son's first aim.

I shook myself, & burst into giggles. I'd been reading about animal behavior patterns, searching in the mating rituals of other species for further examples of my husband's lack of conjugal cooperation. My reading must have filtered into my thoughts. Although I thought that I was not thinking   anything at all   at the time. That my mind was a blank.

The 3 hippopotami gave me an idea, which I presented to Laius: Why not include his beloved Chrysippus in a love triangle on my couch? He is tempted because Chrysippus is tempted. Laius is heralding a time when men will reproduce with each other, without any need for the power-draining female abyss.

Meanwhile, female power will be at its apex tonight. We have a glorious full moon. & on Gamelion 26! The alleged wedding night of Hera & Zeus. Quite an omen for conceiving a new life.

Laius is counting on sowing a son into my unavoidable abyss.

CHAPTER 3

I'm pregnant! Irrefutably. Already visibly. I feel restored in the recognition of my biology. It may be my selfish imagination, but it seems to me that the good people of Thebes are heaving a sigh of relief.

Laius & Chrysippus have driven off to Delphi, to consult the Pythoness about the future of 'their' son.

I said to Madame Tiresias that: 2 negatives making a positive, my child might well turn out to be a girl. She hushed me. I will have a son: she declared: It is the will of the gods.

Very well: I said: I shall be pleased with whatever comes out of me. Even if it looks like Chrysippus.

Her face became a mask of horror, & she shuffled from the room. She makes me laugh; she's such a prude.

CHAPTER 4

On this, the 24th day of Pyanepsion, I gave birth to a splendidly healthy, perfectly formed little boy, with intelligent eyes. He looks very much like me.

Perhaps having 2 fathers favors the mother: I said to Madame Tiresias. Whose face froze up. I do enjoy shocking her with references to Chrysippus' stimulating presence at my child's conception. I'm thinking of naming him Chryses or perhaps Chrysaor in honor of that golden stimulation . It should please Laius also.

I'm ridiculously happy. & surprised. I didn't expect to find such joy in motherhood. I used to think breeding was the fulfillment of less intelligent women. Now I think that the body has an intelligence all its own.

CHAPTER 5

What kind of beings are these wizened virgins Apollo appoints to sit astride tripods, & predict human misery from the mists of sulphur fumes? Do they envy motherhood for which they are too old, even if they were to break their vows of chastity? Do they hate children? Do they hate humanity?

Is this yellow-eyed hyena aware that she is murdering a beautiful, now forever nameless baby with the venom of her words? Does she remember what she said when she comes out of her trance? & asks for water to relieve her throat? & perfumed lotions, to relieve the sulphur stench. & combs to comb her spastic hair?

I feel like confronting her myself. Not in consultation. I want her to see my empty arms, from which a bright new life was torn, & handed to a messenger of death, because of her drug-induced mutterings. To be murdered, instead of growing up to be a murderer. A parricide.

Allegedly, infants don't suffer death as keenly as adults. They haven't been in life long enough to have learned fear. That is Laius' miserable consolation to me. I shouldn't give the child a name, in my thoughts of him. I'm only personalizing my grief.

At the audience tomorrow morning I am to tell my women who will tell all of Thebes that the heir to the throne succumbed to crib death, during the night. & that his parents are too bereft to hold city-wide mourning

ceremonies for him. One look at my face should convince
them that the child is dead.

He blames me now   my idea of our threesome with
Chrysippus   for inseminating me with his murderer. My
nameless little son would grow up to kill him, & marry
me, if he believes in the ravings of the tripodded mambo
mouth.

Did she, too, read about father-killing, mother-mat-
ing young hippopotami? It all makes no sense. Either:
Laius believes what the oracle said. In which case, killing
his   & my!   son defies the plan of the gods. It's dis-
obedience. & ultimately an act of disbelief. Or else: Laius
does not believe her. In which case: Why kill my son!

Madame Tiresias is pacing around my bed with a face
that says: Stop dissecting everything. You're too intelligent
for your own good. Whatever that is supposed to mean.
Meanwhile, a perfect child is being put to death. I dare not
ask by what barbaric means.

Perhaps they'll drive a thick thorn through his new
little feet & hang him upside down from a tree, for birds of
prey to feed on. Our poor do that sometimes, to get rid of
yet another mouth to feed. I torture myself with that
image.

I said to Laius: If the prophecy had been that our son
would murder his mother, & become his father's lover, I
would have let him live. Just to see if the oracle told the
truth. He shrugged, smug with his averted murder threat.
I can no longer bear the sight of him. We're obviously not
going to lie together again   with or without the stimulating assistance of Chrysippus   for the rest of our   now
presumably prolonged   life together.

Madame Tiresias says: That chastity preserves a youthful figure, & complexion. Which is grotesque, coming

from a woman who looks the way she does. Which I
didn't say to her, of course. Instead I said: I thought it
brought with it a certain acidity. A tightness of the lips, &
yellowish skin.

She didn't answer me. She was hovering over my
son's emptied bed, literally scanning the still-warm cloths
with her watermelon breasts. Until I asked: What she was
doing?

Feeling for the baby's lifespan.

But my son was dead.

Not just yet.

I grabbed her wrists: What did she mean? Was there
a hope that he might survive his murder?

Instead of giving me a straight answer, she pulled
away from me, & started holding forth about hope. &
about fear. The 2-fold seed of doom. Both were an error
in time.

Whose error?

The error of us mortals, impatient to know what lay
ahead.

I burst out laughing, hysterical with grief. What a
self-defeating thing for a seer to say!

Not at all. She'd be only too glad if people stopped
asking for predictions. Which they then tried to prevent
from coming true.

So that's what she was looking for in my son's bed.
She was checking up on her rival in Delphi.

Not a rival. Far from it. A dedicated seer, who always
spoke the truth.

How could that be? My husband lived. & he'd just
killed my now forever nameless son. —As well as any
feelings I may have had inside me. For either of them. I,
too, had been killed tonight.

Not just yet. I still had many years ahead of me.

I wasn't looking forward to a son-less life. Married to a child murderer.

The oracle did not speak of infanticide. Fear always made itself come true.

What was she saying! How could a helpless infant foil an attempt on his 2-month long life?

The gods would show me how, in good time. With that, she shuffled from the room.

Chrysippus was so shocked by Laius' selfish cruelty that he quietly packed his bags, & drove his chariot out of town, on the same night, perhaps at the very hour, that my son was carried off to slaughter. I find myself phantasizing that Chrysippus took him along, cloaked in the protection of vicarious fatherhood.

Laius' grief   for his lost lover, far more than for the son he ordered to be killed   gives me little consolation. We live frozen, parallel lives inside our childless palace. Each going through the motions of our respective tasks of government. Our paths seldom cross, & when they do, we politely step aside to give the other right of way. Often we end up retracing our steps. I've sent word to my brother Creon, to take up residence in the East wing. To mediate our solemn silence during mealtimes. I have nothing left to say, even to myself.

CHAPTER 6

The 24th day of Pyanepsion: My nameless son would be 18 years old today: I said to Madame Tiresias, who came shuffling toward me in a straight line. Unseeing, & very fast, like a hurled object, rather than a person walking.

I had startled her. She gave a muffled cry, & then I saw it happen. Right there before me. She turned back into a man. The melon breasts flattened. The hairline rearranged itself, receding at the temples. The bristly old-woman's moustache that shadowed the upper lip expanded into a beard of a softer, lighter texture. The bluish-white layer of blindness seemed to thicken over the eyes. The figure grew in length & shrank in width. He violently shook for several minutes. Sighed deeply, bowed to me, & shuffled on toward his rooms. —Which the servants fear to clean, because of the snakes he/she keeps there.

For 7 years Tiresias stays a man. Aloof, yet everpresent, like the air around me. A silent witness to my daily life. A stern spectator. Then, for another 7, the breasts are huge. The eyes less glazed. The hair looks thicker on the head, & sparser about the cheeks & chin. Now, once again, an adolescence later, Tiresias is a man.

I don't know which I prefer   or resent less: the voluminous woman, or the brittle, blinder man. Neither of whom I find particularly aesthetic.

I asked him later that afternoon, when he'd finally come out again, wearing different clothes: Which sex he found more comfortable to live with, having experienced the shortcomings & advantages of both.

Mainly the shortcomings: he sighed. But then conceded that life was less restrictive for a man, within the 7 gates of Thebes. For one, he was not expected to be seductive.

How rude of him. But …I was curious: I said: During the 20 or so minutes of transition   from male to female, for instance   was he able to impregnate himself, like the androgynous snail? Then bear & nurse his child, & mother it during the following 7 years as a woman? Was that how his daughter Manto had come into being, since no mention was ever made of his daughter's mother?

He shuddered. The transitions felt longer every time. & increasingly painful. He imagined his serpents felt similar pain during molting. Which was why he had taken to rubbing the crowns of their heads, to loosen the last point of contact between the old skin & the new.

Pain left no margin for arousal: he assured me: To him, the thought of arousal mainly recalled the one transgression of his youth. When he'd glimpsed Athena nude, bathing   as he had been   in the river. An inadvertent glance he didn't even have the time   or the experience to expand into lust. For which the goddess struck him blind. Shocking any fantasy of sex out of his mind & body.

His daughter Manto had been conceived during a dream. In which he was a young man, still able to see, and allowed to appreciate the divine beauty of a woman with masked eyes in her late 20s or 30s. Whom he eventually recognized, in his blindness, retracing his growing daughter's beautiful face with his hands. He was not at liberty to reveal the woman's name.

Apollo fell in love with his daughter which had worried him at first, recalling incidents of divine vindictiveness whenever Apollo felt spurned. But the god had remained kind. Watching over Manto as she bore & raised the son she conceived from the union: the brilliant seer Mopsus, his illustrious grandson.

Later, Apollo conferred the gift of prophecy to Manto as well. Now his daughter was one of the unerring Pythonesses in Delphi. It was quite possible that it was she who transmitted the oracle about my son to King Laius.

How awful! I'd always pictured the Snake Lady as a dowdy elderly female with a strident voice. And now he was telling me that she was beautiful. And his very own daughter. I preferred to continue thinking of her as anonymous. Personalizing one's enemy only inflated one's hatred.

He shrugged: I'd asked about his daughter, and he had told me.

It occurred to me that Tiresias & I hadn't talked in all these uneventful 18 years. I asked: If this afternoon's conversation meant that the gods were getting ready to play their parlor games with us again?

If they were, blasphemy was not the way to deal with our fate.

How then were we to deal with it?

We should live virtuously, as though we could improve upon our lives, knowing all the while that we had no say in the matter.

I found that most unfair.

Yes: he sighed: He used to think that his blindness was unfair, too. Until he realized that not seeing the details of life made the divine groundplans visible to him.

I can't imagine how seeing misery before it happens can compensate for a flowering almond tree, or sunlight fractured in the prism of an amethyst. Unless one derives satisfaction from the suffering of others, or superiority from knowing what others still ignore. Which I can't

imagine Tiresias does, as a man or as a women. I didn't ask
him any more questions.

Not even if he knows why the Sphinx suddenly
materialized outside our city, flown in from Ethiopia on
her eagle's wings. What she may symbolize, with her
bullish chest, her lion's tail & paws, & the giant head of a
woman. She intercepts every able-bodied young man who
crosses her path, & asks him a riddle. Devouring him when
he fails to solve it. As has been the rule so far, our young
men's minds being less agile than their bodies these days, it
seems. I haven't met anyone who has the intelligent eyes
that looked into mine from the bed of my little nameless
son, before Laius had him taken away.

Laius is planning to drive his chariot to Delphi once
again, to inquire ...of Tiresias' daughter?... how to get rid
of the nuisance from Ethiopia. I don't understand how he
can go back there, after what she told him the last time.
Unless he feels the wretched woman saved his life, allowing him to murder his predicted murderer. He's letting life
get in the way of living is how I feel about it.

Since that self-preserving night   & the departure of
his beloved Chrysippus   my husband has turned into a
fanatical hypochondriac. Extending the constant preoccupation with his survival to everyone around him. Including horses & dogs. He views us all as potential sources of
infection. Even the cattle he's so proud of. He selected a
group of some 100 men who make the rounds of our city
every day, with limejuice-soaked strips of cloth tied over
their mouths & noses, to check on the health of every
family. The Health Spies: our people call them. They're
afraid of them. Of their half-hidden faces, & the merciless
efficiency with which they cart off the unhappy sick. To a
large boxlike building Laius had put up outside the city
gates   Hades Hall: is the popular name for it   where they

lie around. & sometimes get well, but usually get worse & die. The corpses are instantly burned, & the ashes dumped into a segmented stone trough behind the building. Each section is sealed off as soon as it is full.

The sick try to hide their symptoms until they collapse, or are denounced. Often by a health-conscious servant, or family member. Their brainwashed grandchildren.

In the beginning, many of the rounded-up attempted suicide by rolling themselves off the carts at a sharp bend in the road. Then kept rolling from the road down to the sea. But Laius soon put a stop to 'germ carriers infecting our water'. Now the Health Spies fasten nets over the cargo on their carts.

Radical measures beget radical reactions. I watch our citizens seesaw between ruthless greed & selfless dedication. In both cases, their actions often result in death.

Laius is particularly upset by a small group of men & women who make it their task to clean & feed the helpless inmates of Hades Hall. Quietly defying his neurotic quarantine. Some among them know about the pain-numbing properties of certain plants, which they administer to the sickest in the form of potions, or pellets. Last week, a wealthy old man was killed along with his pain. After leaving his house   which has 22 columns!   to his potion-dispensing caretaker. In gratitude, & in writing.

Laius seized upon the incident to proclaim that our sick are being cheated. A) of their possessions that should be left to their surviving kin, or, if intestate, to the City. & B) of the death to which they are entitled. Death must not be made too easy for us: he declares: It must be the conscious culmination of how we have lived.

A rather provocative statement to make, for a believer & oracle consultant, in my opinion. Apt to tickle the

imagination of an idly listening god or goddess. But his
philosophical rantings are, of course, only a pretext. To
rationalize the posting of sentinels around his ugly building. Rude men with half-hidden faces, who strip-search
anyone coming in or out.

Since last week the Health Spies are also supervising
the eating   & especially the drinking   habits of our
healthy population. There now is a fine for keeping more
than 1 amphora of wine in a household of 4.

& they prod the sedentary   like our contemplative
Tiresias, or my brother Creon who likes to chronicle
rituals, & explain their reason for coming into being, as a
collective outlet for emotions that might otherwise foster
malcontent & subsequent rebellion   to get up from their
couches & take brisk daily health walks around the inner
city.

Needless to say: Bribery is booming. The Health
Spies & their informants are getting quite fat. But that
doesn't keep my husband from thinking of himself as a
benefactor of our people. A 'hygienic ruler'. He disgusts
me more each day. Especially when he borrows my polished silver panel to study the coating of his morning
tongue. Which looks obscene to me, no matter what its
color. I can no longer hear him pronounce the word:
Health, without wanting to vomit. Of course I don't. I
don't want to become queen of Hades Hall. With my
tunic knotted tightly between my legs. Which is what our
sick women have started to do, to keep their private parts
private, during the bumpy ride outside the city gates.

Shame begins where beauty stops: Laius declared
sentenciously, upon hearing of the recent practice. Elabo-
rating on the vanity of women: One foot in the grave, yet
still concerned about their hemline. Ha…Ha…Ha!

   Until my brother Creon pointed out that the women were hoping to prevent   or at least to delay   getting raped by the Health Spies. Who were becoming true health threats, a strip of cloth across the face offering no protection during sexual intercourse. Now our hygienic ruler is threatening to castrate all rapists.

   Creon, meanwhile, has become fascinated with fashion as a prelude to the mating ritual.

CHAPTER 7

Decidedly: the gods are at it again: I was awakened in the middle of the night by our chief runner, who brought me the news that Laius had met with an accident on his drive to the oracle. On the rocky, winding road half a day's distance from Delphi. The breathless man said the King had been dragged to his death by the suddenly shying horses of his own chariot.

I'm having my brother Creon organize mourning ceremonies throughout the city. Every household will be issued white fabric for robes, & ashes. Which   he assures me   purge the surviving of resentment.

It hasn't worked for me during all these years. I've dressed in white   without the ashes, but discarding all jewelry   mourning the murder of my son. But my resentment has grown deeper with every day. Against his murderous father. Against the oracle. Against the gods, playing games with our mousetrap lives to alleviate their immortal boredom. Taking bets on if & how we'll chew our way out.

I look beautiful in white: my attending women tell me every morning, with the sincere flattery that qualifies them for their office. White sets off the darkness of my hair & eyes. & every morning they look sincerely shocked when I reply that it sets off mainly the darkness in my heart.

I dismissed the runner, to take a meal & a bath, then sent for Tiresias. But Tiresias pleaded a headache, & refused to come. I felt that my need to know was greater than whatever pain he was having, & rushed to his rooms.

He was lying on his couch, surrounded by a nest of snakes. The room was shrouded in darkness, which struck me as an exaggeration, for a blind person. & I said so.

His skin became painfully sensitive to light when he had a headache: he moaned: & his serpents were molting. Light was painful to them also.

I apologized for bothering him. & them. But I needed him to tell me if Laius had died of an accident, or if he had been murdered, as the oracle had said.

Murder *was* an accident: he said wearily. Barely audibly: Just like conception was an accident. The geographical coincidence of 2 people, brought together by the gods in a given place, at a given time.

2 people! Was he implying the presence of a murderer then?

Why did I keep asking what I had been told before?

I hadn't been told anything. I hadn't consulted any oracle. I didn't necessarily believe in pestering the gods with questions. But Laius did. & had. & obviously believed enough in what he'd been told to make quite sure that the unwelcome prediction could not come true.

But if it had come true   somehow, despite all his precautions   if my husband had indeed been murdered as the oracle had said he would be   —& by whom he would be!—   well, then I might start believing in the Pythoness myself.

Please! Couldn't he make a little effort! All I wanted him to tell me was if I should look forward to seeing my son again soon.

Tiresias was writhing on his couch, mumbling that he could tell me nothing I didn't already know.

& suddenly I knew! The oracle was fulfilling itself.

Certainty spread through me like the early spring sun beyond Tiresias' drapes. Flooding my being with long-forgotten warmth.

It was unkind of me to tease the suffering man on my way out. Inquiring: If I should send the Health Spies to his rooms. But I felt exuberant, suddenly. Most unbecoming for a recently widowed queen. That's what faith does to the believer: I teased myself: It projects a direction onto the drift that is life.

I sometimes wonder if Tiresias is grateful for having had his life extended to 7 generations. Which strikes me as a rather dubious godsend, especially when it's not accompanied by lasting youth & health.

CHAPTER 8

Thebes teems with ash-smeared faces above fluttering white robes. Creon's dream of the perfect mourning ritual has turned into a nightmare for our treasurer. At every street corner, tables have been set up, with food for the poor, & not so poor. Whose ash masks of grief look to me constructed around a secret smile.

I passed an old woman clutching an amphora to her breasts like a cherished child. The age-watered eyes shone with a deep joy; under the ash the face was radiant with the anticipation of tasting the wine.

Except for the Health Spies whom we instantly disbanded every one seems relieved to mourn a king 'who died of too much health': as people are joking in whispers. —They're joking even about the formidable Sphinx, standing guard outside Hades Hall. Whose in-mates are feeling better, being fed roast goat & lamb by their dedicated little group of potion distillers. Who are pouring them cups of wine. The entire city feels rejuvenated.

Perhaps only to me. As I try to rejuvenate myself, in preparation for the much younger husband the oracle has promised me.

Creon has issued a proclamation that awards my recently widowed hand to whoever vanquishes the Sphinx. Who but the young parricide with the intelligent eyes: if I believe the oracle. & I do. I really do.

I know the prophecy was meant to be a curse. Un-

fairly hurled against an unwitting child, & selfishly enforced by the child's father. But the child's mother is
determined to turn the curse into a blessing. 18 unhappy
years are tragedy enough in any mortal's limited life.

That's why I'm offering lavish sacrifices to Hera,
during the mourning ceremonies. Which surprise   but do
not displease   Creon. Gems & perfumes, a basket of her
sacred pears, my best embroidered belt. One of the horses
that dragged Laius to his death. —Whipped on by whom:
I no longer need to ask Tiresias. It whinnied outside the
gates, sweat-streaked & wild-eyed; it, too, programmed by
the gods.

I am Hera's highpriestess, after all, & she protects
wives & marriages. & is herself the sister of her husband. A
much closer tie, genetically, than a mother & her son.

May not the curse have been turned back upon itself
when my gods-fearing husband sacrificed his son to his
own continuation. Thinking up ever more pointless measures to protect his royal life   making life miserable for the
rest of us   for 18 endless years?

While my estranged son grew toward his appointed
fate: as the murderer of a stranger who was probably
denying passage to a young man journeying on foot, on
the narrow rocky path, which the royal chariot with the
lion emblem filled to capacity. Perhaps a tilting chariot
wheel ran over the young man's foot. Which was still
sensitive from an old wound, perhaps made by a thorn
driven through his crossed feet, when he'd been a baby.
When the unknown man he killed   —in reaction to the
sudden pain that stirred a dark memory perhaps; in rage &
self-defense, & fulfillment of his fate—   had tried to
prevent that fulfillment by killing his 2-month-old son.

Who would not have murdered his father, if he'd
known that the man in the chariot *was* his father. If

he'd been allowed to grow up in daily familiarity with his parents, like a normal child.

Who would not now be on his way to wed his mother.

Might Hera not see the convoluted logic of it all? & decide to absolve my son for killing an arrogant, ill-tempered egotist he did not know?

& look kindly upon the offerings of her highpriestess, who is imploring her divine protection for this predicted second marriage? About which husband & wife have no say, since it is ordained by the gods.

CHAPTER 9

I've been sitting before my polished silver panel all morning, studying my face. Not out of vanity, or sudden self-
doubt, like an actor's dread at the opening of a new play.
—The tension allegedly heightens his performance.—
I don't distrust my desirability at this point in my life. I'm
of that certain age intelligent young men are often drawn
to. & find alluring. Feeling better understood than by girls
of their own selfish youth, that is still blunt like the horns
of young deer.

I'm convinced that a woman close to 40 & a man
soon to be 20 make an ideal couple. —Their difference in
age compensating for the greater importance our society
has begun to accord to men.—

At least the ideal couple is the image I wish to project
to my people. I want them to think of my new husband as:
a brilliant, beautiful stranger, who freed us from the Sphinx.
A perfect new mate for their widowed queen, whose
happiness will leak down to them.

But I worry that the more observant among my
people might begin to notice an uncanny resemblance
between their queen & the stranger, as they watch them
drive   or walk   side by side through our city streets. On
display during the wedding ceremonies, that will follow
the mourning ceremonies almost without intermission. A
sameness of look in the eyes, for instance, that cannot be
smiled away as the body gratitude of newlyweds.

Which may prompt the older among my citizens to

count the years since the alleged crib death of the royal
baby. Whose arrival they'd all so anxiously awaited. Whose
natural death they'd never quite believed, right after the
old king's return from consulting the oracle. & figure that
their new king & heralded liberator must be about the
age that mysteriously dead royal baby would be by now.
& revive dark ugly rumors. Prompting the jokers among
them to start snickering about: a marriage made on
Olympus...

I am an intelligent woman. & I intend to use my
intelligence not only to embrace my fate with my eyes
wide open, but to seduce it. I want my second marriage to
become a model of harmony & enlightened co-rulership.
The secret desire of future generations. I will add to
Creon's mating rites of fashion by changing the look of my
eyes, in case the eyes of the bright, beautiful stranger still
look very much like mine.

—After looking at a totally different life, for 18 years.
At different sceneries, & people. Which may have influ-
enced his looks. Perhaps environment moulds our features
more than kinship. But I can't count on that.

I keep wondering where he grew up, & how. In
another city, or among shepherds, or peasants somewhere
in the countryside? Was he raised by fishermen near the
ocean? What may be his social class? His education? His
manners?

So many questions. Some of which will answer themselves, by the way he'll enter our gates, & greet us. & tell us
how he did away with the dreaded Sphinx.

The other questions I plan to ask sparingly, through
long years of happy cohabitation. Never letting on that I
may know the answers more truthfully than he does.
Which he must never know, in case he is conservative,
like most daring young men. Who believe in the moral

justification of our various social taboos.

Marriage taboos the strictest among them. —Which seem moral even to my amoral outlook when they restrain an impetuous father from forcing himself upon an adolescent daughter. Who is ill placed to withhold her consent. As is the younger sister of a lustful brother. A mother   or a sister; any female   is less empowered to force her desires upon a son, or a brother. On any man, whose flesh would have to be somewhat willing   it seems to me   to achieve inbreeding. The subject of the taboo.

Which allegedly produces deformed or feeble-minded children. Although the gods seem to do it with impunity. No taboo was invoked when Zeus married his sister Hera. & brothers are traditionally marrying their sisters, in the royal families of Egypt. Without any evidence of deficient offspring. —Perhaps because the marrying siblings are all superior specimens.

As I am. My father Menoeceus is one of the few surviving men who sprouted   in full armor   from the dragon's teeth our City's founder Cadmus sowed in Boetia, the Heiferland. Sometimes I feel a streak of dragon deep inside me giving me the strength to continue to be. & my son was a perfect baby for 2 happy months of my life.

& we purposely inbreed our dogs & horses   our sheep   when we wish to emphasize a mother's particularly valued trait. Mating an exceptionally intelligent bitch with the strongest male in her litter. A swift mare with her colt. A golden-fleeced ewe with her lamb.

I shan't have recourse to the luckless parsley to abort a child that may grow inside me after fate mates me with my son. Certainly not the first child, the test child, whose mind & body will reflect the further intentions of the gods. If he   or she   is beautiful & bright, & of a smiling disposition, I will know that Hera lifted the curse the oracle intended. & I will sacrifice to her every day of my remaining life.

Meanwhile I have destroyed the potential detection of the curse, by changing my appearance.

There's an Egyptian among my attending women, who paints her eye lashes the color of her river at home: Nile green. I've had her paint mine, but blue, which I consider more in keeping with mourning. The result is quite startling; slightly Sphinx-like. A total transformation.

Creon squinted at me for the longest time, then asked: What it was that made me look so different?

I told him I was wearing my widow face. It was my elaboration on his ritual of mourning. Which   I thought ought to begin with the eyes.

He approved enthusiastically. A splendid addition. It defined the eyes, yet made them look mysterious. Like held-back tears. He hoped other women would follow my example.

I hope they will. —& that my son will defer his hero's welcome long enough for our people to get used to my new face. I wish I'd believed in the oracle as soon as Laius told me what Tiresias' daughter had said. It would have given me 18 years to work on developing a lack of family resemblance.

CHAPTER 10

Fate seems to use time in a way that defies human calculation. Perhaps the gods enjoy rushing us to the point of frenzy, then keeping us waiting until we feel forgotten. & start asking their oracles once again: What they really have in mind for us? Did we perhaps misunderstand the first time? Were we perhaps misinformed by a husband who feared any male child of his as a threat of replacement?

10 days have passed since I received the news of Laius' death. & painted my eyelashes blue. 10 days is a long time for a healthy young man to walk a distance our chief runner can do in 18 hours. Even if the young man's feet are sensitive. & were perhaps injured during his encounter with the ill-tempered stranger, together with his pride.

Perhaps he hesitates to enter a city, whose ruler he drove to Hades. But he doesn't know that the man he killed was the ruler of Thebes. A Theban, perhaps, if he recognized our lion emblem, but not necessarily the king himself. Even so, he must realize that any city would welcome anyone who got rid of the Sphinx outside her gates.

If nothing else, hunger should urge him on. Although perhaps he's used to sharing the frugal meals of shepherds, & likes to linger in their company. ——UNLESS: he has himself become the latest meal of the Sphinx!

Which is what I asked Tiresias this afternoon. I sent

for him, when my anticipation turned to worry. & my worry to obsession.

He appeared at once, as though he'd been standing behind a column of the throne room. But instead of answering me, he said: He had been told about my painted eyes. & how our fashion-conscious women were all imitating their queen. Why was I painting my eyes, if not to fool a family resemblance with my predicted suitor? Since I'd suddenly become such a believer, when my husband's predicted death came true.

I had expected my predicted suitor sooner.

Had I not begged the gods for extra time, to get Thebes used to my changed face?

Yes. & I was grateful. But 10 days...!

He was a young man, wandering through a Thargelion landscape, abloom with young nymphs & shepherdesses. Could I blame him if he was late for an appointment with his mother?

I hushed him in terror. He was never   & I meant: NEVER!   to speak of that relationship, if he valued his cushioned existence in my palace. That relationship was a divine secret. Between the gods & me. & I intended to keep it a secret until the moment of my death.

The gods might not feel bound to that exclusive secrecy: he said: But...very well...he would feel bound to it, since it was my wish, & I was his queen. —But perhaps my ostentatious offerings had pleased Hera so much that she'd placed a lovely young shepherdess on the wanderer's path. Who watched him vanquish the Sphinx, & was now winding flowers into his heroic hair, telling him how wonderful he was. Until he lost all desire to travel on to Thebes, & decided to stay with her forever, & marry her, & raise sheep, & little shepherds & shepherdesses.

No!

No? Well, then perhaps the Sphinx fell in love with his intelligence, when he solved her riddle, & instead of drowning herself she was now carrying him across the ocean, back to Ethiopia, where they would live happily ever after in mythful bliss.

I demanded that he stop his nonsense.

Nonsense? Had I not implored Hera to turn the curse into a blessing?

But not like that. What about *my* fate? How dare he mock me, his queen! Was this supposed to be a retaliation, because 10 days ago I'd called on him in what I considered an emergency? Thinking that the death of my husband was more important than his headache, & his molting snakes.

Suddenly, the sleepy afternoon palace came awake with voices & running feet. My women rushed in, ahead of Creon, who led a dust-clad stranger up to me.

This is Oedipus: he announced: the son of King Polybus & Queen Periboea of Corinth. He freed us from the Sphinx.

I rose to my feet, a gracious queen, welcoming the liberator of her city.

He no longer looks like me at all. Nor   mercifully like his deceased father.

CHAPTER 11

Our treasurer is trying to argue Creon out of giving a city-wide week of banquets —each day to be centered at 1 of our gates— to celebrate my wedding to our liberator & new King-to-be.

Who walks in on the discussion, unannounced. Scrubbed, & smelling like a cloud of musk blended with roses. Looking very regal, in that ornate Corinthian style our men here may find a trifle too decadent to imitate.

He slightly surprises us all, when he instantly sides with the treasurer. Declaring that: A whole week of free roasts & especially of free wine will debilitate the citizenry. Who'll need twice as long to recover from such unaccustomed high living. Creon's generosity is not only a waste of existing funds, it also jeopardizes future work energy.

Our treasurer beams & nods. & complains about the further outlay for fabric for festive gowns to be issued city-wide, just after the recent issue of fabric for robes of mourning.

Our liberator & King-to-be instantly questions that need: Why new fabric? Why whole new robes? Why not simply give them colorful ribbons, which the citizens can affix inventively to their mourning dress? It will be an incentive to their inventive spirit. To the artist that dwells inside all of us...

Our treasurer praises the idea. I can see nothing

wrong with it myself. Creon shrugs: All right. But his eyes
are pleading with me for arbitration.

So I say: Our liberator's modesty is admirable. Most
auspicious for his & my co-rulership.   —At the word:
co-rulership, his eyebrows rise, & his eyes harden.—   But
surely, having been raised with the principles of government in his mother's milk, so to speak, as a royal child in
Corinth, he must understand that rituals & ceremonies
food & entertainment   are essential to keep contentment
among the people. Rituals & ceremonies not only disperse
pent-up emotions which otherwise risk to crystallize into
acts of rebellion, into riots, they're also an incentive to
work better afterwards.

Our people had just experienced the loss of their
beloved king...

He interrupts me: He noticed quite a bit of revelry,
upon entering Thebes. If the bereft people were drowning
their grief, that grief must have been thoroughly drowned
by the time he arrived   as drowned as the Sphinx   to
judge by their high spirits.

Our people are in high spirits, because they're at last
free of the Sphinx: I retort: It would be a political mistake
to dampen their spirits with a shabby wedding ceremony.

The stern finality in my voice surprises everyone,
including myself. I sound more like an exasperated mother,
than like a bride-to-be. & just like a mother, who feels that
she has scolded enough, I switch to endearment.

We're all eager to hear how he managed to do away
with the man-eating monster from Ethiopia: I smile sweetly:
Won't he tell us how he was able to solve a riddle that had
stumped every young man before him. Including my unfortunate nephew Haemon.

He isn't fooled. He knows I'm telling him to change
the subject. To keep his nose out of the affairs of our city,

at least until after he has officially been appointed my co-ruler.

During all my speculations & anticipatory fantasies it never occurred to me that my second husband might disagree with my   or my brother's   decisions. That he might have political ambitions & ideas of his own. A worrisome thought.

It makes me wonder about the relationship he had with his 'parents'. Of whom he spoke at his arrival; with enviable fondness. Had he perhaps been a little too opinionated for them? & was that why he had left Corinth   or perhaps been made to leave?

—Renouncing the throne that would have been his at the death of King Polybus, according to the 'progressive' laws of succession that prevail in Corinth, that pass power & property on to the son, bypassing the line of the mother.

After my airless marriage to a hypochondriachal child murderer, am I about to marry a neo-patriarch? Or is his butting in just the insecurity of youth, trying to make an impression on a new environment?

He obligingly begins telling us about his encounter with the Sphinx. How she loomed before him after the last bend in the road, with the walls of Thebes almost close enough to vault over. But soon he is belittling his undeniable feat, in a way I consider most unflattering to my sex. Intentionally unflattering, to get even with my reprimand, & put me back in my place? Wherever he thinks my place may be.

We're giving him too much credit, he begins. Fixing each of us in turn with a disarming smile. —He has the same white, even teeth Laius used to admire about Chrysippus. They must have impressed me, too, at the very instant I conceived my son.—   We might change

our opinion, we might even think him a cheat, after he
tells us that he has a certain knack that sometimes permits
him to guess another's thoughts. Usually under circumstances of extreme concentration, when he's alone with
that other person. His tutor discovered that he had this
ability   this gift from the gods   when he was 11. When
he answered questions about subjects they had as yet not
studied. When he was able to read the answers in his
tutor's mind.

    & then there was another fact to be borne in mind.
The riddle the Sphinx had asked   —What being with
only 1 voice has sometimes 2 feet, sometimes 3, & sometimes 4, & is weakest when it has the most?—   was not all
that difficult when you took into account that it was being
asked by a woman. What was foremost on a woman's
mind? The obvious answer was: Man. The rest   the
crawling baby / the upright adult / the old man with his
cane   had inserted themselves later, as he thought
about the other predominant preoccupation of women:
Age...aging.

    I squint at him. I probably look annoyed. He smiles
disarmingly, & tells me that: My eyes look very much like
the eyes of the Sphinx before she leapt from the rock.

    Do they really? & can he read in my mind whether
I'm flattered or offended by being likened to a monster?

    The Sphinx had the most mysterious eyes he'd seen
on any female face, until he saw me. & he's looking
forward to reading my mind as soon as we're alone together. When he hopes to read the same thing that has
been on his own mind since the moment he walked into
the throne room.

    Creon clears his throat: He'll see to it then that the
arrangements get under way for the wedding ceremonies.
Minus new gowns... This wedding marks a new era for

our city, & since the outcome is contained in the seed, he promises me that my wedding will be magnificent. An event all of Greece will talk about & envy.

Our liberator turns his hands, palms up, toward the treasurer. Who promptly imitates the gesture.

I ask: If he would like me to dispatch a runner to Corinth, to invite his parents to the festivities.

He hastily refuses: Even a whole week of celebrations would be over, before his parents could reach Thebes. They aren't the youngest any more. His mother was close to 40 when she gave birth to him.

I don't suggest horses, or litter bearers. His face has become a mask of anguish. I shall definitely ask about his relationship with his parents as soon as we're alone.

It will provide a pretext for not allowing him to lie with me just yet. I want to build his desire for me, & prolong it. It will be a typical 'woman's' revenge for belittling her sex, when he belittled the intelligence of the Sphinx.

I must discipline my mind not to think anything I don't want him to know. That should be quite a lesson in self-awareness.

CHAPTER 12

Thebes, this first day of Thargelion

To: King Polybus & Queen Periboea of Corinth

Most Beloved & Respected Parents:
I hope this finds you in good health; usefully occupied as
always. Too busy to worry about your wayward son, who
misses you both very much.
A great deal has happened to me since I last embraced you,
on that windy Gamelion morning, when I set out for
Delphi to consult the oracle about The Gods' intentions
on my behalf. I never thought that I was embracing you
for the last time.
You must believe me: It is not a lack of filial affection that
is keeping me away from you. It is something the oracle
said. Which is too dreadful to be believed. & unrepeatable.
Nothing could be more alien to my mind & nature.
Yet, we are told that the oracle at Delphi never lies. &
since I did consult the woman, I feel that I must listen to
her, & make quite certain that what she said to me will
not   CANNOT!   happen. Unhappily, this means that
I may not see either of you again. Not for a long time.
Perhaps never.
At first I felt that my inevitable decision   to journey ever
further away from home, from Corinth where I was born
& raised   would break my heart. How could I go on
living without your loving guidance? Dejectedly I wandered along my lonely road. Withstood insults & humilia-
tion heaped upon me be a stranger traveling in the oppo-

site direction from mine. Then found my path blocked
by…no other than The Sphinx. I thought my end had
come, & I rejoiced. Perhaps my resolve not to go back to
you was allowing me to die with my innocence intact.
But when I was able to solve the riddle The Sphinx was
asking me — easily, as though prompted by The Gods—
I felt that They were satisfied, now that I had heeded Their
warning. & was sacrificing all that I held dear in life. That
my test was over, that They absolved me & were now
leading me toward a new life, filled with new challenges &
responsibilities. Even new love.
As a reward for vanquishing The Sphinx, & liberating the
City of Thebes   —You know: 7 gates; Lion emblem.
Quite a busy place, though no Corinth—   I am about to
marry the City's recently widowed Queen. Her name is
Jocasta. She seems to be extremely religious   —a highpriestess of Hera—   & quite an autocrat.
Indulgent only of her brother's wasteful whims. I'm re-
minded of what you always say, Father. About displays of
piety as a cover-up for abuse. Their economy seems quite
shaky, yet they're planning a whole week of ceremonies
for this wedding. Of course it may have been the dead
king who emptied the treasury box. I don't think he was
very popular. The mourning ceremonies for him looked
like drunken brawls to me. Perhaps he was ill. Or very old.
They had no children.
Well, I'm planning to change all that. —Yes, Father:
Quietly, without making waves. Even if you named me
for the cresting sea.— I've already won over the treasurer
by suggesting how to save on fabric to be issued for festive
gowns. & I'm counting on winning Queen Jocasta over
with love. I feel that she's quite attracted to me. I like her
also. She's beautiful, in a strangely stylized, remote sort of
way. Perhaps your son has fallen in love?

Dear Parents, how I wish that you could be with me during this unnecessarily expensive week of celebrations, following on I don't know how many days of mourning libations. But you MUST believe me: It is essential that we remain apart. It is the command of The Gods. I will write to you as often as I can. Jocasta gave me a generous supply of linden bark to write on, & Thebes has a fine team of runners. I miss you both. I miss the simplicity of my young life between you, when doing what you told me to do was all I needed to be good. The Gods express Their wishes less simply. They told me what to do by telling me what not to do. Or so it seems to me. I hope I'm Their obedient son as much as I am your everloving

OEDIPUS

P.S. Dear Father: I will do my best to be a just & compassionate ruler of Thebes. Like you, I plan to walk the city streets incognito, listening to the voice of the people for my performance report.

P.S. Dear Mother: Would you please give my musk & rose mix to the runner to bring back to me. I've used up the little flask you gave me to make myself presentable to my Queen. Thank you.

Œ

CHAPTER 13

This is the First Day of Thargelion
Day One in the Reign of King Oedipus
of Thebes.

& may it be a very good day to you, too, Old Walrus. You won't believe what you got me into, with your stupid taunts about how I don't look anything like my parents. Insinuating the gods only know what about my monogamous mother having done it with one of them. No, Walrus, not with Hephaestus. That does *not* explain my nose, thank you.

But then again, maybe you saved me from the most disgusting predicament ever thrust upon an unsuspecting son. Do you remember how we laughed about what that ever-indignant Academus taught us about animal behavior. A young male hippo, killing his sire & mounting his delighted mum. We laughed so hard, he threatened to inform my father of our disrespect.

Perhaps it is to punish me for my irreverence that old Academus somehow got the oracle   —a great-looking lady, by the way—   to predict that same ridiculous fate for me. —But why only me?   Why not you as well? Because I'm the hero! Ha! & you're supposed to be my conscientious chronicler...?

With all due affection for dear old mother, I can't picture myself getting it up for her, or with her, not even with the help of dungheap mushroom fantasies. As to the old man, why would I want him out of the way? I liked my life the way it was. I was in no hurry to inherit his throne. He's a good king. I admire him, even. Yet, that's exactly what I'd be doing: the oracle told me in a puff of sulphur breath, I'd be slaying the old man, & bedding down with the old lady. Can you beat that!

No way was I going to let that happen. So I decided that I couldn't return to Corinth, to the 'soft life' you always ribbed me about. I hit the road as a beggar. A real beggar, mind you, not a king's son in disguise. Anything rather than risk turning into this freak. This parricidal motherfucker.

NOW LISTEN, WALRUS: UNDER NO CIRCUM-STANCES DO YOU TELL ANYBODY ABOUT THIS ORACLE, YOU HEAR! AT LEAST NOT UNTIL AFTER I'M DEAD...IF YOU SURVIVE ME....

Okay, so, sure enough, beggar treatment is what awaits me the very next day. A man in a chariot comes riding down the road toward me. His horses shy, & what do you think the bastard does? He threatens me with his whip, & won't let me pass.

Well, you know me as a peaceful sort, who'll put up with a lot to avoid a fight, but there was something about this arrogant guy towering above me on his chariot that really got to me. Before I knew what I was doing I'd jumped up beside him & was wrestling the whip from his fist. His horses dance like crazy, the chariot tilts, & the guy falls off. I jump back down myself, & resume my humble beggar's road. I've no idea what happened to Mr. Right-of-Way. I didn't bother to look. I hope I taught him a little more courtesy the next time he encounters a peaceful beggar traveling on foot.

—Half a day later, one of his horses comes tearing past me. I guess he drove on with just one horse.

I looked a sorry mess, let me tell you. Clothes ripped. Legs, arms & face caked with sweat & dust. I was also getting hungry. This is now a week later, give or take a day. I'd

eaten up what I'd taken with me. I could see city walls in
the distance. So I thought I'd take a dip in the ocean, to
make myself a little more presentable before I walk through
the gates & start asking for work. As a scribe, or a perfume
maker, perhaps.

But a bath was not what the gods intended. Suddenly there
is this thing standing before me   this monstrosity   this
SPHINX. Looking at me with the most fabulous eyes.
Eyes that freeze you on the spot. She has an enormous
woman's face, the rest is claws, & paws, a lion's tail. & she
speaks just like a woman. Caressing, silky-voiced, she asks
me a riddle. & when I solve it for her   or maybe the gods
solved it for me, now that they're reconciled with me for
not going back to Corinth   the eyes become even larger
   early-morning blue with night-black centers. She lets
out an earsplitting shriek, & hurls herself into the sea.

I felt utterly drained after solving that silly riddle, & must
have fallen asleep right where I stood. When I wake up it's
dawn. My legs are in the water, & something is bumping
against them. It's the Sphinx again, but now she's quite
dead.

I pull myself together. I wasn't going to bathe in the water
next to a female corpse. Necrophilia isn't my thing. Dirty
as I am I stagger toward the city. Which turns out to be
closer than I'd thought. From Academus' geography lessons I realize I'm in Thebes. But I think I'm hallucinating
after I walk through the gate   —unimpeded; there's no
one there to ask my name, or question the purpose of my
visit—   & find myself surrounded by drunks. At mid
morning, people are lying across the streets, snoring. Others are weaving about, gorging themselves on roasted
meats, & washing it down with wine. Some of them
directly from large amphoras, tilted above their mouths.
Not even bothering with cups.

Famished as I am, I head toward the nearest food table, &
help myself. There seems to be food set up at every street
corner. What's the occasion? I ask an old woman who's
hugging an amphora to her breasts like an illicit lover.
The king is dead: she grins: We're mourning our king.
Before I can ask why she sounds so happy about it, heavy
hands clamp down on my shoulders, & there behind me
stands the guard who should have been standing at the gate
when I walked in. This is the man! he shouts. He killed
her! I saw him do it! He killed the Sphinx! Now we're
free of her. We're free…
Suddenly the foreign beggar has become a local hero.
Hands reach out to touch me   pet me   shove bits of food
& cups of wine into my face. How come I'm alive? the old
woman wants to know: How come the Sphinx didn't eat
me up? She likes succulent young men.
I guess I was too scrawny & dirty for her: I laugh. Thinking: Had I known that she might devour me, her riddle
might not have been quite so easy to solve. Fear getting in
the way of reason. They all laugh with me. I'm their
liberator. Their hero. Now I must marry their queen, &
become their new king.
You know how drunks talk. I could have been a real
beggar, without any preparation for rulership, it would
have made no difference to them.
I need to take a bath before I marry their queen: I say.
They laugh, but they're determined. 6 younger guys hoist
me on to their unsteady shoulders, & off we trot to the
palace, followed by a teetering, yelling mob.
I'm deposited in a room filled with women. The queen's
attendants. Most of them great looking. A lot better than
the dignified attendants of my homely little mother, that's
for sure. Then I see the man they're all clustered around. A
seated, solitary man with a lemon face, who turns out to be

the queen's brother. Creon. Bureaucratic, & full of himself.

His face brightens when I tell him who I am. That I am the son of a king, that is. My name   or rather my age/my youth   seems to give him trouble. Oedipus? he drawls: Oedipus? He hopes that doesn't mean that I have a swollen head.

I was borne into life on the swell of a wave: I tell him. With the 'gracious politeness that is the first prerequisite of rulership': as our ever-indignant Academus never stopped telling us. & as my mother used to tell me at least once a week. I know the brother doesn't like me. I feel it. One of those infallible first impressions.

Luckily, the queen is not at all like her brother. —See, Walrus: even siblings don't necessarily have a family resemblance!—   Although she seems to like him a lot & indulge all of his whims. All of them wastefully expensive. Another infallible first impression: She's attracted to me. Love at first sight?

Her eyes are out of this world. Heavily painted. She looks like something I might have picked up myself, if I had the guts. She's a little older than what I might have risked. A bit forbidding. Hardly the sweet young thing a son brings home to his parents. Rather the kind of mistress you might introduce to your father, some night when he's taking you out on the town to show you the ropes. & you show him that you know those ropes already. I'd feel more comfortable as her lover, than as her husband. But her husband I am, as of tonight. Such is the wish of the gods now that they've scared me enough to stay away from Corinth for the rest of my life.

Are you envious again, poor old Walrus? You always wanted to be me. But you're not. I'm the hero, you're the observer. My chronicler. Which gives you freedoms I have

not, believe me. You'll learn to cherish them someday, as you start writing up the history of the judicious reign of the greatest, most equitable King Thebes ever had.
Your old pal
                    Oedipus

Whose incomparable feats will follow in regular reports. I have all the linden bark to write on, courtesy of my generous queen. Whose name is Jocasta, by the way.
& we have a fine team of runners. —Make this one wait for a letter from you back to me. That is a royal order! & treat him well, he's a fine athlete.
We also have a regiment of charioteers, consisting solely
    get this!   of lovers. Every driver is the lover of another driver in the group. A regiment of pederasts. It was the dead king's creation & claim to fame. He proudly proclaimed himself the first pederast in all of Greece. I guess that explains why he & my queen had no kids.
REMEMBER: NOT A WORD TO ANYONE ABOUT WHAT THE ORACLE SAID TO ME!
I didn't invite you to my wedding celebrations, old Walrus, because I'm severing all bodily ties with Corinth. Just to make sure. I'm not taking any chances. I miss you, though. I'd just love to see you swallow hard at the sight of my queen.

CHAPTER 14

Oedipus has been writing letters all night, instead of making love to me.

I was going to let him in at last, after 6 long nights of lying side by side. Desire lying between us like an obstacle, across which we seduced each other with our eyes   our hands   our lips & tongues   our toes   groping and grasping   doing everything but the final, total thing. Which   I said   had to be saved for the 7th night, until the ceremonies were over, & all of Thebes had gone to bed, after he had officially become my husband.

I didn't even laugh when he chided me   paradoxically respecting me   for: being very religious; very conventional.

Now he's writing endless letters to Corinth, about me, I imagine, to keep me waiting in turn. To get back at me. The obviousness of his strategy is touchingly juvenile. & effective.

In a way, though, I'm grateful for the reprieve. Despite my sincere contempt for man-made taboos & religious scare tactics, something dark inside me balks at the prospect of letting Oedipus reenter whence he came forth into the world.

Many times, during these exhausting nights of stayed seduction, I felt on the brink of hinting that I know who he 'really' is. But he doesn't doubt that he really is Oedipus of Corinth. Oedipus of Thebes only as of tonight. & can I be sure that he always was Oedipus of Thebes?

That he is indeed the unlikely survivor of my dead husband's precautionary measures? That he already fulfilled the first half of the predicted abomination he thinks he's running away from by not returning to Corinth —If that is why he did not return to Corinth after consulting Tiresias' daughter?—   & is now about to consumate the second half, whenever he finishes writing his letters.

Why would he believe me, if I told him that after being hailed as the liberator of Thebes, he should now stand trial for the murder of her king? Do I know for sure that he met   & killed   Laius before he met & killed the Sphinx?

Whom he actually did not kill. Who killed herself when he solved her riddle.

Ironically, I find myself mourning for her. I grieve that female intelligence is currently being perceived as a monster that must be slain.

The Sphinx was not mentioned by the oracle 18 years ago. She wasn't part of my son's scenario. Could that mean that Oedipus is *not* my son, after all?

During those 6 long nights of stayed seduction I asked him about his journey. Guardedly: Had the road been much traveled, this pretty spring season? Had he met anyone interesting…other than the Sphinx?

He smiled into my eyes, telling me nothing. He didn't wish to be distracted from our desire games.

I asked: Why had he left Corinth? Had he not felt happy there? Had he perhaps quarreled with his parents? About the succession, perhaps?

I had offended him. Only a matrilinear-thinking mind could come up with such a ludicrous notion. His parents are   & always will be   what he holds dearest in his life. —A little stab in my direction: I am not what he holds dearest.

Then why did he not wish them to be present at our wedding? I stabbed back.

My questions have spoiled his mood. Moreover, they're gratuitous. As Tiresias told me: Why do I keep asking what was answered 18 years ago? But once again I'm no longer sure of anything. The sudden belief that flooded me at Laius' death ebbs & crests, & ebbs again.

When I first heard his name: Oedipus: I was sure my horror fantasy of the thorn-pierced baby feet had been the gruesome reality. That Laius' torture tactic had left him swollen-footed. The first time we were alone together, I inspected his feet   the soles, the insteps   under the pretext of a love massage. I found no scar, not even a healed, closed-up puncture point.

I asked how he got his name, & he told me: His mother was close to 40 when she was pregnant with him. He was her first & only child, & was giving her intolerable labor pains. Finally, her attending women carried her to the ocean, & seated her with her back to the waves. The first incoming wave brought him forth. He was the son of the Cresting Wave.

It sounds possible. More plausible than the ruse of a childless royal couple happening upon a 2-month-old baby on a beach, after it survived being thrown into the sea. —Perhaps at the same spot where the Sphinx drowned herself.— A baby that floated the distance from Thebes to Corinth unharmed. & now, 18 years later, the survivor, the adolescent hero, walks back the distance from Corinth to Thebes, to fulfill his fate in my bed.

If that is the implausible truth, I still have time to stop it. At least the second act of it. I can wait up for him, & tell him that we need to talk.

CHAPTER 15

For hours I lay on my couch, looking at the night. Rehearsing what I should say to him. Projecting his reactions: Would he believe me? & if he did, would I lose him for a second time? Only worse than the first time? Would he run from me in revulsion, hating the bad mother who had done nothing to protect her helpless child? & was now seducing her adolescent son?

It was almost dawn when I heard Oedipus summon the runner. I got up to watch the man set out. At that mechanical-looking trot, that seems quite slow. Whose speed is always a surprise when he arrives. Then hurriedly I lay back down, & pretended to be asleep.

Another hour must have passed before he finally tiptoed in. Smelling of the hyacinth I use, but mixed with something harsher; a little tangy. A very pleasant, though somewhat overpowering scent. Which he had invented for me, for our wedding night.   —Which was practically over.—   It smelled strong enough to wake the dead, but I remained asleep. & he believed me. Or pretended to. Perhaps we were both pretending, trying to win the waiting game.

Besides, I was feeling a touch of irritation, after waiting most of the night. During one of our desire games, he had criticized my perfume as being too sweet. I was no spring flower: he had declared: I needed to cut the hyacinth with something aromatic & slightly harsh.

I was impressed that he knew that I was wearing

hyacinth, which is a rather exclusive scent. & since he seems to take smells so seriously, I asked: Why   did he think   the Pythoness shrouded herself in sulphur stench? Why would the evocation of truth require an evil smell?

His answer impressed me even more. Sulphur: he said: was the smell of fear. He had definitely smelled it once, on a man whose whip he was wrestling from his fist. It was the smell of fear for our life, the fear that drove us to consult the oracle. The Pythoness used the smell of our collective fears to induce the trance that permitted her to translate the plans of the gods.

It would have been the perfect moment to ask Oedipus if he had consulted the oracle, on his way from Corinth to Thebes. &/or to tell him about the oracle of 18 years ago. But I let it pass. I let him resume our desire game with the passion of an adolescent determined to be a good man.

He slipped under the covers beside me. I was lying on my right side, my back turned toward him. Sleeping more deeply than ever. Unstirred by the hand that was gently resculpting my shape. By the voice that was whispering into my neck that: I was his sweet, old fashioned tyrant. Whom he would subjugate with love. The Corinthian style of love, that knew how to treat women the way women secretly longed to be treated. With the firm, loving hand a good man used with his dogs & horses. Because women were animals at heart.

He whispered a detailed list of harsh things he planned to do to me as soon as I woke up. Eventually he whispered himself into a climax against my sleeping lower back.

After a while another kind of lukewarm wetness fell against my sleeping neck. He was weeping, whispering: How much he loved me. All the more for having saved him from the horror told him by the Sulphur Siren in Delphi. Who had called him: A wretch, who would slay his father, & couple with his mother.

I lay stiller than any true sleeper can lie, & only after he had whisper-wept himself to sleep, did I softly turn around & take him in my arms.

& then I, too, must have cried myself to sleep. Crying over my helplessness before the will of the gods. & my guilt, of complicity with their will. While my body basked in gratitude for being loved. For feeling love again, for the first time in 18 years. A deeper   requited   love. For the first time in my almost 40 years of life I was given a mate. I was no longer alone on this earth.

When I woke up, it was a golden morning. Oedipus was still lying in my arms, but awake, loving me with his eyes. Wordlessly, our smiles reached out & sealed each other. Our nipples touched. Our bodies fused. We stayed joined for many hours. Falling asleep together, waking up again.

We're offering Hera a young golden ram, to protect our new marriage. Oedipus will perform the rites, wearing my priestess robes. We think Hera will like that. All women in their prime like being served by worshipful young men.

CHAPTER 16

Every day, a new pain in a new place teaches me another lesson in anatomy. I know precisely where my liver is located. My bladder. My prostate gland. At the same time, my senses are sharpened to intolerable keenness; mainly for unpleasant sensations. My ears wince at a raised voice. My skin crawls at the touch of a hand that is cold or moist or inordinately hot. The garlic I eat to keep my blood clear has begun to nauseate me with its smell. The wafts of perfume that hail King Oedipus' passage through the palace take my breath away, & make me choke. —I hesitate to think what the palace in Corinth must smell like, if that's the fashion there. If he's a product of his upbringing, rather than a rebel.

The smallest draft gives me a stiff shoulder. When I misjudge the height of a seat as I sit down, lightning shoots up my spine, giving me an excruciating, lasting headache. Immobility cramps my legs, yet walking makes them ache. My toenails are growing into the flesh of my toes; I can no longer reach them to keep them trim. More & more I need to rely on service from others to maintain this bulky body, that has become old & ungainly in either sex. That clamors for its due, & imposes retributions, if my mind focuses on matters of its own. & I'm only in the 6th of the 7-generation lifespan the The Gods granted me to compensate me for the loss of my eyesight.

I do not question the wisdom of The Gods. Obviously I need the experience of prolonged deterioration to

achieve indifference to physical discomfort, & lack of
aesthetics. To my ugliness: I may be fortunate not to be
able to see what I've grown to look like. I crave detach-
ment from it all. Equanimity. Which I obviously have not
achieved, as long as I crave it. I'm a slow learner, unjustly
credited with wisdom by the royal court of Thebes. Where
I'm kept as a mouthpiece of The Gods. My grandson
Mopsus is far wiser than I. He was born wiser. & my
daughter Manto has grown wiser also.

I doubt that either of them would let Queen Jocasta
get on their nerves, with her endless questions. Varieties of
the same question she has been asking me for the last 19
years. At any time of day or night. Regardless of how ill I
may feel. Making sport of my various ailments. Which
would be a royal tragedy, if just one of them should assail
her royal body. She hears my answers as reprimands, so she
slightly modifies her question, & asks again. She'll keep
asking until she hears what she wishes to hear. Which I'll
never be able to tell her: That she may continue to do as
she pleases, & will be applauded for it.

Even by The Gods. Whom she thinks she can bribe,
with her sudden sacrifices. After ignoring Them for close
to 40 years of her life. Suddenly she's eating pears, Hera's
sacred fruit.

I might have firmer grounds to implore The Gods
myself: To restore my sight. To allow me to remain in the
same sex, preferably the male sex, into which I was born.
To reduce my lifespan to normal duration, or else rid me
of my pains. I never neglected my devotions, either in
thought or in deed. & my eyes were innocent. They never
intended to insult Athena's Mighty Chastity. But Queen
Jocasta imagines that The Gods will listen to her   instead
of *her* listening to *Them*   because she's the Queen of
Thebes   of superior stock. & intelligent.

She may be all of that   apparently she's also still quite beautiful, at almost 40   but her intelligence is focused on detail; it neglects the total image. Life, to her, seems to be composed of isolated occurrences. She's like another experience of blindness to me, when she fails to understand that no good can grow from a poison seed.

Which was sown the night she persuaded King Laius to copulate with her, with the assistance of his lover Chrysippus. The golden horse-youth, who pleased the queen as well. —Who pleased even me, when he let the blind old woman I was at the time scan the classic contours of his face with my hands.

King Oedipus was the child of human willfulness, a conception enforced against the plan of The Gods, Who had decided to keep the royal marriage barren. The queen would have done better to copulate with Chrysippus alone, in frank adultery. The Gods are known to acknowledge the purity of flesh's passion. To smile on a child of lust, but not on calculated defiance. Oedipus was not meant to be born. Not any more than his unfortunate sons are meant to be born. Being also his brothers.

With all her vaunted royal intelligence, the queen would do well to study my serpents. From a single elegant undulation of their streamlined bodies, she might learn where to insist, & where to yield. But the queen doesn't like my serpents. She's afraid of them. Or feels superior to them, because they symbolize the waning half of the year, & she proudly identifies with the lion   her City's emblem which represents the waxing half. People derive feelings of superiority from the oddest circumstances, that are totally unrelated to personal merit. Of course my serpents pay no heed to such matters. They're wisely indifferent.

Which I ought to have become by now, after 6 generations of human experience, in both sexes. But I still

find indifference difficult to achieve   & harder to maintain   as I sit in the palace garden, soaking up the midday
sunshine of yet another early   lion   spring with my
parchment skin. I smell the hyacinths I vividly remember.
I imagine their midnight blue, their icy white, their sunset
magenta.

Suddenly, their scent thickens chokingly, its sweet-
ness cut with an aroma of herbs. I smell the perfume King
Oedipus invented for the queen.

Who thuds down on the seat beside me. 10 months
have gone by since Oedipus returned to Thebes, & the
queen is about to give birth, becoming a grandmother in
the process.

Oh Tiresias: she pants: I feel like a pugilists' arena.
Pummeled by a barrage of tiny fists & feet. Am I going to
have twins?

I nod.

Boys? Or girls? Or 1 of each?

Twin boys.

Why are they so belligerant inside her? Do they hate
each other, already in the womb? Or are they just healthy
& energetic, impatient to come out into the world?

I shrug. I have no answer she would want to hear.
She'll find out soon enough what kind of unfortunates
she's bringing forth this time. What does she expect,
knowingly copulating with her son, despite explicit warning from The Gods!

My un-serene heart goes out to the unwitting son,
the unwitting brother of his twin sons. My king. Another
intelligent human being, who thinks he can outsmart The
Gods. Who thinks that he has, in fact, outsmarted Them,
when he did not return to Corinth. But unlike his father,
he knowingly harmed no one but himself, when he re-
nounced his royal station & decided to live the life of a

beggar, rather than commit the crimes my daughter told him he was about to commit. He doesn't know that his decision not to return to Corinth was the first step in the direction of those crimes. Which he has been perpetrating every day ever since. Lovingly. With the best of intentions. He wants to be a good man. A good king. A good husband & father.

Wafts of musk & roses herald his breathless arrival in the palace garden. He is bringing his queen a pain-numbing potion he has concocted to ease her labor. He will not leave her side until it's all over. Until he can be sure that mother & child are doing well: he assures her nervously.

She tells him: That I said they're going to have twin boys.

The information increases his nervousness. He takes a sip from the bitter-smelling brew he brought for her.

He seems to know a great deal about potions, & lotions. I feel like asking him for something to soothe the pulling in my ever-colder legs, that are running ahead of me into death. Of course I say nothing. How could I presume to distract him from his queen's impending delivery. Which worries him. All the more since he believes that it is her first time, & he knows she's not the youngest, despite her cunning cosmetics to disguise her age; along with tell-tale family resemblances.

I clumsily rise to my swollen feet, & shuffle off, my ears repelled by their royal bedroom cooing. As I reach my rooms, the unfortunate twins are being slapped into life. The entire palace complex is shaking with their screams of indignation at having to be.

CHAPTER 17

When the first phase of the oracle fulfilled itself with Laius' death   —shocking me into believing in oracles as voices of the gods—   I made a covenant with Hera: If a child of mine with my miraculously returned son came out of me with a healthy mind & body, & a serene disposition, it would be her sign to me that she   & the other gods at her persuasion   had reversed their curse. That Laius' murder by the son he'd tried to murder had evened the divine scales, & they were ready to look kindly upon my 2nd marriage, which they had brought about, spinning skillful webs of human intrigue & misunderstanding.

Their kindliness toward my marriage is indisputable. Thank you, Hera, Benevolent Benefactress. I could not wish for a more thoughtful husband. An inspired, yet yielding co-ruler, who is leading our impoverished city back to prosperity.

& I certainly cannot wish for a more inspired, yet yielding lover. I think   in fact: I know   that Oedipus has become addicted to making love to me. He wants to make love to me not only every night, but during the day as well. We'll be sitting side by side in the throne room, giving audiences. Hearing grievances   —to which he always seems to find an equitable solution. The moment there's a lull in the succession of petitioners, his strong young arms scoop me up, & carry me off to the nearest couch.

My women have begun to throw me probing looks. As though to ask: If I possess a magic charm which they might borrow, or steal? They flirt with him outrageously, openly hinting at their own availability. They can't believe that he's not interested, when he smiles deeply into their painted eyes, & sends them off to run errands for him. To take a new fortifier he has concocted   —a mixture of goose blood, egg yoke, & spinach juice—   to some anemic child in the poorest section of our City. Where my women have never set a dainty foot. Where they get mud on their golden sandals.

He laughs with me about their disappointment, & tells me that: I'm his addiction. The more he lies with me, the more he wants to lie with me. Touching me every-where. Scratching me. Biting me. Then soothing the an-gry spots with the warm wetness of his unshrinking desire. Slowly, as in a dream. Leaving glistening snail trails along my inner thighs. & from my navel to my neck. To my mouth.

He looks forward to us being old together: he says   —as though unaware that I'll be quite old when he'll still be quite young—   when our children are grown, & able to take on the duties of government. When we can spend all our time on the couch. Separating only to heighten the thrill of reconnecting.

He wants me to puncture him with sharp little bites, to make him feel that he has fallen into a hedge of thorns. He wants me to ride him while impaled, & gyrate until I collapse on top of him. Bending the pale at an odd angle. Making him feel that it has broken off. He readjusts his position, & penetrates me so deeply, that I faint. A dead weight, I lie on top of him, pressing the air from his lungs, until he faints also. Our spirits rise from our bodies, & sail away on the moonbeam of united ecstasy. While our abandoned bodies sink ever deeper into each other. So deep, that no one can pull   or tell   them apart.

This has been our daily life, for 16½ married months. Miraculously, I'm never tired, or indisposed. We made love until the very end of my pregnancy. Until Oedipus could feel our child inside me box with him. Which   he said   gave him added pleasure. But then, as soon as the twins came out, & I recovered from their exit, he hurried back inside me. Saying: How much he enjoyed having me all to himself again. Without protest from my 'tenants'.

Since the birth of the twins, he remains inside me when he falls asleep. I have grown to like it. It makes me feel anchored. The confines of my former self have melted. The royal we truly describes the single   total   being we have become. I want to say: Yes! to every sensation, to every aspect of life. Except to the dark secret at the pit of my being.

But I don't know what to say about our twins. What to make of them. Oedipus delivered them himself. Unwilling to let anyone else reach inside what he calls: My secret door.

Eteocles came out first, literally kicked out by his brother. Polyneices. Who then took his time about his own emergence. As though he wanted to be alone in the fleshhouse that is my womb. An only child, for the 12 minutes it took to pull him out. This is what Oedipus tells me. I was unconscious from the potion he made me drink at the first flash of pain. It made me feel so relaxed, I thought I was a gate that Hera was opening. & there my thinking stopped.

Apparently I slept through the delivery. & continued to sleep for many hours afterwards. When I woke up, I was surprised that it was dark. That my belly was flat. Decorated with a beautiful brooch   silver braided around gold that was lying on my navel. A birthday present from our twins: Oedipus said.

Suddenly I became aware of a chorus of screams bellowing from the nursery. Apparently it had been going on since the moment they were born, with interruptions only for feeding. Oedipus thought the wetnurse might need help, & went to investigate. He came back laughing: He'd found 2 tiny warriors, furiously kicking & batting at each other inside their crib, screaming themselves purple.

He had them placed into separate beds, & the noise abated somewhat. But as soon as they sensed each other's proximity, at feeding time, the screaming started up again.

Now they are in separate rooms, at far ends of the palace, with a separate wetnurse for each one.

I've been thinking: How do the women of the people raise their children? In limited living space, & still working the fields?

Our twins are almost 4 months old now. They're healthy & beautiful   unusually alert for their age. Ready to smile at everything & everybody, except at each other. Whenever they're brought together, they start screaming, straining toward each other with fiercely raised little fists. Oedipus thinks they're very funny; he's looking for a teacher to give them boxing lessons. He thinks it's natural for twins to resent each other. We all want to be unique. He's fascinated watching them fill in their personalities: he says: Eteocles heading toward true glory, & Polyneices toward much strife.

But my ever-vigilant dread is rising in my throat again, as I wonder what kind of sign, what kind of divine message these boys are meant to be. I've taken a basket of the year's first pears to Hera, keeping only 1 pear for myself, to share with Oedipus.

I've also asked Tiresias: What he sees lying ahead for our little pugilists.

As usual, he responded with a lecture. This time about: 'Knowing the seed'.

I thanked him. I knew this particular seed. I knew it intimately. It was my knowledge of the seed that had prompted my question.

Then it should also provide me with the answer: he sighed, & shuffled off to his snakes.

He has been using a cornel staff lately, to supplement his jellied legs. His tapping on the palace floors sounds like the erinnies, timing a taboo breaker on the run.

He always makes me feel stupid. Perhaps I ought to give him the pear I set aside for Oedipus & myself. Perhaps that will sweeten his answers in the future. The gods aren't the only ones who like to be bribed.

CHAPTER 18

Being the only one to know the guilty secret of the incestuous queen has forced me into an unwanted complicity with her. Against my wish I'm made to share the shameless sham of her married bliss, which she rationalizes endlessly   to herself & to me   with self-serving examples from animal husbandry, then tries to ensure with exaggerated sacrifices.

In the solitary confinement of her knowledge I'm her only link with reality. The hired ear she fills with her worries & her doubts. Abusing her royal station to importune me with almost daily requests for reassurance, which I'm in no position to give. Usually during my favorite sunshine hour on a bench in the royal gardens.

Lately she has been trying to bribe my cranky impartiality, or perhaps my continued discretion. Moving me to the south wing of the palace, where my age-brittle bones & my serpents enjoy added warmth. This afternoon she brought me a rare pear, to coerce me into listening to her current inner turmoil, as she is about to give birth again. Her worried mind keeps projecting the kind of omen the new child will be: she tells me: At the same time she worries that her worrying may flaw the child, & the omen.

Anticipating the worst neither stays nor precipitates it: I say, biting into the pear. The juice runs into my balding beard. I probably look repulsive to her. She's probably sorry she gave it to me.

She's still afraid to trust the Benevolence of The Gods: she sighs: even though Hera seems to be smiling on her marriage to Oedipus. She worries that it may not last. Every time he wraps her in his strong young arms, a voice inside her says: Oh...but...if you knew... His love feels undeserved. Fraudulent. She wishes she could tell him.

Sometimes she's sure that he knows, or at least suspects. But loves her nonetheless. All the more, since they're accomplices, in a world peopled with judges. That he'd say: Shhhh!..., were she to tell him. Cautioning her not to let words denounce the social taboo they've been breaking, in silence, every night & mostly every day, for 2 happily married years. —Do I think that a social taboo may not be a taboo, in The Eyes of The Gods? After all, Zeus is Hera's brother.

I mumble ignorance, munching my pear.

Of course, by social notions, they're living a precarious fraud. But their love is authentic! Should that not redeem their union, & purify them both?

I shrug. I have little experience with love. Which is all too often confused with lust.

Yes but... not in *their* case. Theirs is a total love. It has overcome the separation of individual selfishness. She feels that it has made her a better person. She has become more understanding, much more caring & giving. & don't I think that Oedipus is an able, caring father & king? Remarkably practical for someone only 21 years old.

I nod. & thank her again for the generous pear. Which I've eaten peel and seeds. Now I'm chewing on the stem.

Even her brother Creon   —who doesn't particularly like her husband, as I must have noticed. I must have noticed that they're pretty much staying out of each other's way.—   admits that Oedipus has been good for the City's economy. The people are content. They're eating their fill.

I nod.

Do I think that means that The Gods have revoked Their curse of 21 years ago? Or have they just forgotten about them?

I shrug. I don't know. All I know is that divine timing cannot be measured in human years.

She's aware of that. But does that have to mean that fate is running its original accursed course, undammed toward damnation? That will engulf her, Oedipus, the twins, the new child in her womb, maybe all of Thebes?

I shrug again. I repeat that: I don't know!

If her marriage to Oedipus breaks a taboo also in The Eyes of The Gods, what punishment should she expect? She knows of no precedent to their case in the Annals of Divine Justice. Of no punishment fixed for it. Do I think there may be no punishment, other than her constant fear of revelation?

I don't know. Perhaps.

But in that case, what about Oedipus' punishment? If he doesn't know or suspect what he has done, how can he be punished with fear of revelation?

Yes, how indeed?

Oh, I'm no help at all!

What does she want from me? That I let the king in on our secret?

He walks in on us at that point, & starts kissing her like a hungry puppy attacking his food. She kisses him back, oblivious to 'the blind man'. I don't wait around to hear what other indecencies are about to follow. I shuffle back toward the south wing, appended to my blessed cornel staff.

I'm doing fine! she calls after me, suddenly remembering my existence   her recent transformation into a more caring person   I should keep it up!

I feel like roaring an outraged NO!!! I feel like asking her: If she'd tell Prometheus that he's doing fine, chained as he is to the Caucasus. That he should keep it up, as the eagle pecks at his liver. Of course I don't. She's the queen, dispensing charity to a cranky, ungrateful old seer. I shuffle on, eager for the uncharitable elegance of my serpents.

CHAPTER 19

Our little Antigone is 6 months old today. She slipped out of me causing me barely the slightest discomfort during the night of the winter solstice. Heralding the Return of the Light: Oedipus says. She's an undeniable stamp of divine approval. I'd be an ungrateful wretch, if I still doubted that my second marriage is pleasing to the gods. Anyone who looks at our little daughter feels joy.

Even the twins stop their war cries in her presence. They waddle toward her on their still bowed, unsteady legs, unclenching their little boxers' fists to touch her cheek with the gentlest care. Beaming as though caught in a ray of sun.

—Their resemblance grows uncannier every day. They really look interchangeable. Oedipus had 2 arm clasps made for them: a golden lion's head for Eteocles, & a silver serpent for Polyneices, to help us tell them apart. I suspect them of switching their clasps when no one is looking, to confuse their nurses. Oedipus says: Perhaps they think they're switching each other. That Eteocles wants to be Polyneices, & Polyneices wants to be Eteocles, at least for a day. Their precocious cleverness never ceases to amuse him. His love for me, & those who come out of me, is Hera's most precious gift.

I've created a miracle: he says: Antigone is so beautiful & sweet. Exactly how he imagines me to have been, when I was 6 months old. I have miraculously recreated myself.

I don't quote what I've read about breeding a mare with her colt, or a bitch with the sturdiest pup in her litter. Nor do I point out that I was a defiant child   a cynical adolescent   a jaded, disappointed adult. That I was far from sweet, until he came   back   into my life. I kiss his mouth shut, & hurry him off to Hera's temple, for another thank-you sacrifice.

We're offering the wide golden armband Oedipus gave me for the birth of Antigone. From Antigone with love: it says on the inside. It looks beautiful on my arm, just above the elbow, but we agreed that Hera must have it. Even if it gets stolen during the night, as all our valuable sacrifices do. Thebes has her network of irreverent thieves, who hide behind the official explanation that: the goddess has come down from Olympus to collect her pickings. They sneer at the curse I placed on anyone robbing the gods. They sell their loot to invisible middlemen, who conduct an underground export trade with equally invisible middlemen in other Greek cities. All of it cloaked in pious respectability.

My awareness of this practice used to keep me from offering valuable sacrifices during my first marriage. When I had only my awareness to be thankful for. Now I feel that, what matters is to give up something you value.

Oedipus agrees with me. He rarely worshipped, in Corinth, but at that time the gods had as yet not intervened in his life. When they placed him on the road to Thebes   on the road that led to me, to my secret door   they changed his life: he says enthusiastically: He became aware of their guidance. Every day they give him new reasons to offer his thanks. Especially to Hera, whose favorite highpriestess I am. Who favors him also, by association with me.

My heart shudders at what he is saying. —He really

doesn't know, then. He doesn't even suspect!— Then shudders again at my lack of faith. Hera's pleasure about the armband   or at least about our readiness to part with it   becomes evident as soon as we return from the temple. When my brother Creon emerges from his 2-year-long seclusion, with Antigone asleep in his arms. He is smiling. He has a suggestion for Oedipus.

I anticipate a hint about spacing my pregnancies, but no. Not at all. He wants to show us drawings of armbands, clasps, & brooches he has been designing. Bold, harmonious shapes, which he proposes to combine with Oedipus' perfumes. He thinks that, together, they might launch an innovative beauty trade. Build Thebes into an export center for luxury items.

Luxury: my brother declares: is an underrated basic need. It is a child of beauty, as important to our senses as food, clothing, & shelter are to the body. Which is the scaffolding for the senses. A useless structure, when deprived of the senses. Whose refinement   through the cultivation of beauty, in art as well as in artifact   precludes the uglifying impulses. Such as apoplectic anger   thin-lipped miserliness   bulbous gluttony. Steeping the senses in beauty inhibits ugly thoughts & emotions. Therefore, selling the ingredients of beauty   the tools of beauty   to the largest possible number of people will not only promote prosperity within the 7 gates of our city, it will spread beauty's message of harmony & peace throughout Greece.

My brother is beaming. Oedipus looks happy, too. They shake hands on their project. Antigone wakes up with a tiny burp of joy.

I don't say that: Wearing beautiful arm clasps hasn't pacified the twins.

As soon as my brother leaves, Oedipus starts looking

through his collection of costumes. He plans to go into town tonight, to check on our people's reaction to the manufacture & export of luxury items. —He, for one, likes the idea very much. What a prompt response to our sacrifice. Hera must have been pleased with her armband. Antigone liked the idea, too. He thinks that little girl is our good-luck charm.

—Once a week, always on a different day, Oedipus goes into the city in disguise. Sometimes he's a bellied grain merchant from the surrounding countryside. Sometimes a pretty young washerwoman. A water carrier. A midwife from Crete. A stone cutter. Every detail of his costume is carefully studied, including the accent & vocabulary that are typical of each trade. When needed, he chips & blackens his fingernails & roughens the skin of his hands. Tonight he's planning to go as a jeweller's apprentice from Athens. What do I think?

I think he should let me go with him. I could be his pompous master. I do a very convincing Athenian accent.

He laughs. He'd love it. But it wouldn't work. We'd give each other away, acting off each other. He, at any rate, would not be able to keep a straight face. He'd be embarrassed, acting in front of me. It would make him feel insecure. After all, he isn't doing this just for the fun of it.

I stare at him. I don't know if it's the way I see him, or his face, that has changed. Suddenly he looks   & even sounds   shockingly like his father Laius, extolling the philosophical superiority of a man's love for another man, or the significance of his regiment of lover-charioteers, which I   a mere woman   can neither share nor understand.

Good! I say in a voice honed with rage. The voice of an indignant mother, whose son is disputing her authority in household matters. Good! Perhaps he'd do well to feel a little insecure. Even without my embarrassing presence. Does he really believe that our people suspect nothing! For 2 years they've been running into midwives from Crete, or stone cutters from Sparta, or grain merchants from Egypt, once a week, who draw them into political conversations over cups of wine. Who draw them out, listening to a problem they happen to have, a complaint. Which miraculously, mysteriously solves itself soon after. Does he not think our people are smart enough to make the connection? I'm not saying that they know they're talking to their king, when they're flirting with a pretty young washerwoman they never saw around before, who disappears into the night, never to be seen again, but I *am* saying that they're pretty sure they're flirting with some- one connected to the royal court   a spy from & for the palace   & that they're slanting their conversations accord- ingly. One should never overestimate the gullibility of the people.

    & just like a son trying to reason with an unreason- able mother, Oedipus invokes the higher authority of his father. Who has been mingling with the people of Corinth once a week for over 40 years. In varying disguises. With excellent results. His father calls that: Feeling the public pulse.

    How does he know the people of Corinth haven't been humoring their king for over 40 years? The same way the people of Thebes have been humoring their new king for 2?

    He shakes his head. He doesn't know, but he seri- ously doubts that anyone suspects him. His disguise is always authentic. He really becomes the characters he impersonates. —Even the female characters. Whom he finds particularly enjoyable. There are more advantages to my sex than most women realize, or are willing to acknowledge. He's smiling. Displaying patience, while I'm being difficult.

Like being pregnant all the time: I say. Being difficult. At least I've wiped the smugness off his face. What do I mean: All the time? I've been pregnant only twice.

I don't correct him. I don't say that: I've been pregnant 3 times. That the first time was 20 years ago, with him. I simply say: Twice in 2 years *is* all the time.

But...he thought I'd enjoyed bearing our beautiful children. He hoped we'd have many more.

I was hoping just the opposite. I was hoping that he'd use his cleverness with potions & perfumes to concoct something   a salve, maybe   that would render sperm infertile. Something to prevent conception. He could market it along with Thebes' new line of luxury items. It would be a huge success. Every moneyed woman in Greece would want to buy it. The midwives could stock it at reduced prices.

We've never quarrelled before, & we're not quarrelling now. Oedipus won't allow it. What a brilliant idea! he exclaims, beaming again. I'm his shrewd economist of fear, suggesting to exploit the fear of giving life. If that really is a general fear among women. He'd always thought people considered their children assets. He certainly thinks of *our* children as glorious little assets. But that is, of course, his male point of view. He promises to work on something...maybe with a citrus base. As long as I promise him at least one more little daughter. One more lovely little Antigone.

I burst out sobbing. I feel totally cut off from this smiling man, who lives his life with blinders on. For which I suddenly respect him less. I envy his blindness, which I don't respect. He takes me in his arms. He asks: If I'm having my period?

No! I'm not. Not everything a woman thinks   &
says   & does   is dictated by her menstrual cycle. My brain
isn't located between my legs.

He's soothing me. Stroking me like a child who
didn't mean to be naughty. Or perhaps like a nagging
mother, who needs to be told that she's still loved. He
won't go out as an Athenian jeweler's apprentice. At least
not tonight.

Predictably, our first quarrel that was no quarrel ends
on the couch. But I'm still angry. Brusquely awakened
from my dream of us as the ideal couple. My body refuses
to participate in his desire, which suddenly feels propri-
etary to me. My orgasm is purely mechanical. I wonder if
this is how most married women feel, after 2 years of
conjugal exertion. If they feel used, as I feel used tonight.
All the more since I'm sure   absolutely certain   that I
conceived yet another child.

The next morning I tell him: I'm pregnant again.

My tone is far from joyful, but he beams at me. He
takes my hands. He kisses my palms. I've made him the
happiest man in the world. Do I think it will be another
adorable little girl? Another Antigone? Another me?

I shrug. He seems to be getting all his wishes. Meanwhile, I have a wish of my own: From this night on I need
to sleep alone.

His joy collapses. His face turns grey. But why? Our
nights have been the best parts of our days.

A mother-body needs more space. It needs the whole
couch to itself.

But I'm as slender as I was 2½ years ago. My hips are
still as narrow as when he met me. & my breasts have
remained the same also, since we bound them so tightly to
prevent lactation. & I won't get big with the new child for
another 5 months at least. & we always made love through

all the other pregnancies. So why not through this one,
when we'll be able to do anything we want to, since it has
already happened anyway.

Do anything *he* wants to, is what he is saying. But I
am saying that I don't want to make love anymore. At least
not for a while.

Don't I feel well?

I feel invaded. Too much motherhood turns a lover
into a parent.

But...what about HIM? he says, smiling sheepishly,
pointing to a little tent his tunic is forming in his crotch.

I'm sure any one of my women will be glad to take
care of that end of the problem.

I wouldn't really want that, would I?

I shrug, wondering how I will feel if he starts lying
with other women. All I want for now is to sleep alone.

All through the day, Oedipus looks crestfallen   —in
blatant denial of his name—   every time he looks at me.
He has been drinking when he arrives   late   for dinner.
Red wine has tainted his shiny teeth a dirty blue. He
continues to drink heavily all through the meal. He's
boisterous, quite obnoxious, telling unfunny jokes that
remind me once again of his father Laius.

Creon shows us several arm clasps the jeweler made
after his designs. Among them a golden dragon I particularly admire. He offers it to me, fastening it around my
upper left arm, slightly above the elbow. It is a beautiful
thing; I make a silent vow that Hera shall not have it.

Oedipus spouts obscenities about the mating rituals of
dragons & dragonesses, which Creon & I try to ignore. But
which rouse my father Menoeceus from his usual peaceful
old-age dinner stupor. Dragons: he admonishes sternly: are
chaste androgynes, who do not mate at all. Twice in their
lifetime they spew a trail of fire, which condenses into a

baby dragon, whom they nurse for as many years as they have teeth in their mouths.

Oedipus laughs. & when my father offers to fight him, he tells him that: He'll have to find himself another midwife to deliver him from life.

Let's go: he says to me: We've eaten enough.

On the walk back to our wing of the palace he weaves alongside me, bumping into me. Outside my chamber I bid him good night.

I can't do that to him! he protests, grabbing my left arm. So hard, the golden dragon cuts into my flesh. I scream, & in a reflex I slap his face. His arm rises in reflex also. I wonder if he gets brutal when he's drunk, like his father used to. My body is not his property: I say angrily: I'm not his chattel. I'm still the Queen of Thebes.

He looks surprised & hurt. His hand has fallen back to his side. Good night, Your Majesty: he sneers, & stumbles off.

CHAPTER 20

This, the 4th day of Skirophorion
an unusually warm day here in
the Fair City of Thebes

Dearest Mother,
I hope that this finds you well, & active, not too much
hampered by the pains in your poor hands. I enclose a
balm for them. Apply amply, despite the odor of burned
feathers. But covering it with a fragrance would diminish
the healing effect. The warmth you'll feel will activate the
flow of blood, & disperse your discomfort. At least I hope
it will.
This letter is exclusively to you, Dear Mother. Not that
I'm trying to hide anything from Father, & if you wish to
discuss with him what I am about to ask you, please feel
free. But it is something I can ask only of you, as a woman.
As you know, my life here in Thebes has turned me into a
believer & a zealous worshipper, having been most amply
rewarded by The Gods after I made the painful decision
not to return to Corinth. I thoroughly enjoy being a
father. The twins grow more identical each day, & more
amusing, inventing new tricks & ruses to vent their rivalry.
Little Antigone is a gem, very much how I imagine my
beautiful Jocasta to have been at her age. I'm truly sorry
that you cannot meet them all. But then: all of life is an
exchange of sacrifices. Perhaps only the wisdom of old age
need no longer yield to fate. Sometimes I feel impatient
for that wisdom; especially when I may be behaving as
foolishly as a young horse.
If it were left up to me, I'd fill up our spacious palace with

hordes of beautiful children. I would love to have many many more. But Jocasta wishes to stop. —& this is what I need to ask you: Do pregnancies & childbearing entail such discomforts & pain that most women would have fewer children if they had a choice?

A slightly older woman, who may be approaching the second half of her thirties? I'm not exactly sure how old Jocasta is. We've never discussed our respective ages, although The Gods know we've discussed everything else on this earth. Her attendants have hinted that she may be almost 40. But they are flirtatious women, not as devoted & loyal as yours. & they are provoked by my fidelity to their queen. Which is not a virtue so much as an addiction on my part. I will be satisfied to love no one but her for the rest of my life. But am I perhaps insensitive to what satisfies her?

& this, dear Mother, is my question: Is it normal for a wife to wish for respite after 2 years of conjugal activity?

Jocasta has asked me: If I might be able to invent something   a potion/a salve   that would prevent conception. She said that 'every woman in Greece would be happy to buy it'. Dear Mother, is this true? Do women bear children mainly to please their men? Or because they have no access to a satisfactory alternative, other than the abortificients the midwives sell? I promised her that I would work on the problem, although not for our immediate own use. I even feigned enthusiasm about inventing such a concoction, although I felt none in my heart.

It is the first time that Jocasta & I do not see eye to eye on an important issue.

I hope I have not shocked you, Dear Mother. & PLEASE do not let this turn your sympathies away from your daughter-in-law, who always appreciates & returns your thoughtful inquiries. After all, the balm I'm sending you any cure, to heal any affliction   is equally an interference with the course of nature. So why not start at the preventive stage, if pregnancy be an affliction?

What I'm asking you is essentially this: Is Jocasta's wish to have no more children natural?

She did have a difficult time carrying the rambunctuous twins, but she did not feel the delivery itself. I'd given her a strong sedative. & little Antigone practically came out by herself, she's such an independent, undemanding little spirit. Jocasta feels that, since we've been married, she has been pregnant *all the time*. She doesn't want to be pregnant any more.

I know you experienced torture bringing me forth. Is that why you & Father decided that I would be your only child? & was it *your* decision, Mother, rather than his? & after you decided, did you practice abstinence, or do you know of some secret formula that made either of you infertile? If you do, I'd appreciate the information.

Please dear Mother, don't think that I'm upset. I'm not. I merely wish to gain objectivity about this matter, & for this I need a woman's point of view. A woman whom I love & trust, besides the point of view of my Jocasta, whom I will continue to love & trust, no matter what your answer.

Otherwise, everything is going great. Thebes' economy is decidedly on the upswing. Soon we'll be completely solvent, to our treasurer's relief. Creon (jewelry) & I (perfumes) are planning to launch a new line of goods   beauty products   which we're hoping to develop into an export trade. I'll be writing you the details, & would of course appreciate the names of jewelers & perfume makers in Corinth who might be interested.

Meanwhile though, Dear Mother, I'm most eager for your reply. I feel that whatever you'll have to say to me on the subject will clarify my problem. Which may not be a real problem, only the impetus & infatuation of my age, & my queen's waning response, fatigued as she may be by too much ardor.

As I said earlier: I love Jocasta. Enough never to touch her again, if that be the condition of our life together. Although touch has been the daily basis of our life up to now. Initiated by me, but always eagerly received & returned, it seemed to me. I know that fire has a life span, but what about the torches that remain lit on our altars, which the highpriestess rekindles in perpetuity? Must it not burn physically as well, to maintain its meaning?

Dear Mother: It is your gut reaction I'm asking for. Forget that I'm your son. Please answer me as though I were Father, wanting to know if he would importune you on your couch. A dreadful thing to ask, for a son of his mother, perhaps. But it's pure theory. So much depends on your reply to me. But then again, it may only be my injured male ego, begging for the reassurance of the norm. Now, Dear Mother, once again: May this find you in the best of spirits. Do not let this letter disturb you, please! I'm grateful for any information   also chemical/technical that you can send me. Your loving & devoted son

                                                     Oedipus

CHAPTER 21

L ast week I had the surprising honor/the honoring surprise of a personal letter from good Queen Periboea, my Corinthian mother-in-law, instead of the usual courtesy inquiries & regards she appends to her lively correspondence with Oe. Her pretext was the birth of Ismene, born on Gamelion 26, Hera's wedding anniversary, & the 23rd anniversary of the night I contrived to conceive my fateful spouse. Ismene came quietly into the world, not unlike Antigone before her, but instead of sunshine she's haloed with sadness. The sadness that is often paired with knowledge. This time I feel that I really reproduced myself. She is another me, & I fear for her.

The good queen mother covered 2½ linden barks with protestations of woman-to-woman affinity   —in a rather minute, convoluted hand—   to conceal   & elicit answers to   2 extremely indiscreet questions: How old am I? & do I feel the need to regain the privacy of my body after the birth of 4 children?   —The 3 preceding ones were not worthy of a personal letter to me, I guess.—

It's a pertinent observation, & none of her business, even if she were the mother of Oe, who has obviously complained to her about my lack of conjugal cooperation.

So far as I know, the good queen was barren. & already elderly when she pulled a 2-month-old son out from under her skirts, passing him off as newly born to her aaing & ooing women, whose professional hypocrisy portrayed sincerest belief.

I feigned similar belief in her motherhood, & facetiously reciprocated her woman-to-woman confidences.
Thanking her profusely for the honor & surprise of a letter
all to myself. & even more profusely for the considerate
husband & devoted father she & King Polybus had raised,
with just the right mixture of love & discipline, an inspira-
tion & shining example for me, for raising Oe's & my 4
Gods-sent children.

—Whom I so wished she could see & get to know/so
regretted she could not see or know. But obviously Oe
had received divine orders to prevent any such meeting,
even though the separation from his parents weighed daily
on his filial heart. He had never told me—had he told
her?—what exactly the oracle had said to him, although
we'd been totally open with each other about *everything*
else. We also worshipped together, which added another
special bond to our unusually close relationship.

We had been drawn to each other, I wrote, from the
moment we met, & even initial differences   such as the
role of the sexes in matters of rulership   had soon
dissolved in harmony & mutual goodwill.

He was such an open-minded, considerate human
being   —for which I could not thank her & King Polybus
enough—   that he now thought of Antigone or perhaps
knowledgeable little Ismene as the future rulers of Thebes,
rather than our rivaling boxer twins. Which I thought
ought to please her: Queen to queen.

Then, ever more facetiously, I spoke to her as mother
to mother. Commiserating with her about the difficult
birth of her only son, brought forth with the help of
cresting waves. Asking if she did not agree with me that,
while it was true that a woman paid a social penalty if she
was barren   —a mean stab at her own penalized state of
22½ years ago—   it was also true that an overemphasis on

motherhood transformed a woman from lover into parent. Furthermore stifling her artistic or intellectual pursuits.

Did she   as I did   marvel at the stamina of the women of our people? How they conceived, worked while pregnant, bore & nursed child upon child while working the fields, & feeding & satisfying their men? I was in awe of these women. Of their faces that resembled dried grapes at barely 30.

I said: How much I admired her & King Polybus' exemplary restraint, having stopped at a single child. Which had permitted her to remain such an effective co-ruler, in a city as modern as Corinth, that favored rulership by men. But the majority of the people could not be taught similar frugality, in matters of sex, their main recreation. Which is why royal couples needed to set an example, & exercise restraint. Did she not agree?

Again I thanked her profusely for the honor/the surprise of a direct communication. Which, I hoped —I hope not!—   would be the beginning of a lively & mutually enriching correspondence between 2 women   2 mothers   2 queens, equally concerned with the welfare of all their children, whether their bodily own or those of their people.

In a PS I asked her: What she thought of the phenomenon of the Sphinx? Exemplifying female intelligence as an enigmatic monster with a predilection for succulent young men. & suicidal when one of them turned out to be as intelligent as she?

Oe has been very curious about his mother's letter. But I wouldn't let him read it. She was speaking to me as woman to woman; it would be betraying her trust. I dropped the 2½ linden barks onto the brazier in my room, & together we watched the flames eat up Queen Periboea's minute handwriting. Her much larger signature stood out in the glow, still traced even in the ashes.

He assumed that I wouldn't let him read my reply either.

I nodded. I'd written back to her not only as woman to woman, but also as mother to mother, & queen to queen. Men had no place in it whatsoever.

Except as the subject: he said. Meaning himself.

I said: No. It was all about women on various levels, & their feelings.

Or lack of feelings: he said bitterly: O, Jocasta, what has happened to us?

I feel as sad as he feels bitter. I'd had such hopes for co-ruling with a man half my age, whose energy & fresh approach   I'd thought   would enhance my experience, & vice versa. A young man who   I'd thought   had inherited my outlook on life, to judge by the intelligence I'd seen in his infant eyes.

I had hoped that, together, we would rebalance the crumbling position of women in our society. Restore it to the natural difference between the sexes, without the recent value judgement that exalts the visible, & abases the invisible to a 'treacherous abyss', as his father Laius liked to call it.

I had not expected to become the focus of a sexual fixation. Which is not an expression of love so much as an exercise in ownership. & as offensive as his father's blatant disregard. It's not worth breaking a taboo for. The strictest of all taboos, that may not only be a law set up by men, but a command of the gods.

On that unhappy afternoon, when Oe explained that his weekly mummeries were too serious to risk my participation, & I suddenly saw & heard how much he is his father's son, I realized that his opinion of women is not unlike his father's either. It closed my body against him.

His obsession with his penis, which   he keeps telling me in an accusatory tone   grows at the sight or mere thought of me, has become as obscene to me as Laius, studying his morning tongue in my silver panel. I can no longer use Oe's name in full, without shuddering at the thought of his swollen organ.

Yes: I say: What has happened to us is very sad. But my secret door slammed shut the night Ismene was conceived. & when she came out from behind it, my hymen grew back. Not in skin, but as a coral reef.

He gives me a long searching look, then runs from the room. Soon he is back, carrying his charioteer whip. I wonder if he plans to give me the treatment a good Corinthian man uses with his dogs & horses. Which women allegedly appreciate, being animals at heart. How am I to deal with it? Do I need to call my women?

But he addresses me in an infantile falsetto voice, handing me the whip. Asking that: His mommy beat him, because he has been bad again. He's a bad boy, always growing hard when he thinks of mommy.

I must look so appalled   Thinking: He knows then! He has known all along!   that he quickly apologizes in his normal voice. Begging me not to be offended. He doesn't mean to imply that I'm old enough to be his mother. He knows I'm much too young to be his mother. This is just a fantasy. A ruse, to get me to touch him again, albeit with a whip.

The petrified wife, who's sitting on my couch   the Sphinx-eyed mother   the Queen of the 7-gated City of Thebes   The Shining Moon   pushes the penitent boy-man off her knees, across which he's trying to lie, to receive his spanking. A hard-eyed erinny has risen to her feet, & orders him to stand by the column at the far end of the room. To bend over. More. To lean forward. The

Erinny's arm starts swinging the whip. Beating the disre-
spectful son who excluded his co-ruler from the fun &
games of government. The arrogant ignorant phallus fixated
on its mother's abyss. Beating my disappointment. & his
blindness. & my inability to get us out of this hopeless
taboo-breaking hole. Until a geometric pattern of neat
pink welts grids the smooth young buttocks, & he cries out
in climax, embracing the column.

He expects me to come running, like a normal
mommy would, to kiss away the hurt she has inflicted. But
the hard-eyed Erinny tells him: To clean up his mess.
Then sends him to his room.

With a racing heart I sink onto my couch. Filled with
shock & self-disgust by the wetness between my legs.

CHAPTER 22

Through the supernumerary years of my 7-generation life span, my hearing has grown increasingly sharper, to compensate for my inability to see the outside world. But an overdue old body makes many strange sounds of its own. My windpipe whines like a child crying somewhere in secret. Full or empty, my stomach growls like an attack dog, ready to pounce. My bones creak like an unreliable bench. I often stand still, to determine the source of what I'm hearing so keenly, afraid to bump into obstacles as I round a column toward my new warmer quarters in the south wing, or feel my way past shrubbery in the palace gardens, until I realize that I'm listening to my own inner turmoil.

My stomach has never sounded like music before, yet music is what I hear as I shuffle toward my chambers after lunch. 2 reeds, engaged in soft conversation. A joyful proposal, answered by pensive elaboration. I pause to listen mainly inside myself   until I'm quite sure the music is outside my body, coming instead from my rooms. Which surprises me: People usually avoid my serpents' lair.

Suddenly, there's Antigone, taking my hand. She hopes I don't mind that she & Ismene visited me during my absence. They've been playing their flutes to make my serpents dance.

& so they are. Undulating about me as I recline on my couch. The girls are sitting at my feet, blowing into their reeds.

I smile, marveling at the merciful versatility of The Gods, growing 2 little hyacinths from cursed seeds. I think of hyacinths, because of the perfume they're wearing, made for them by their father. Slightly different for each girl. I smell Antigone white, or a pale pink, & Ismene a deep deep blue.

They're 12 & 13 now. Soft-spoken, intelligent young beings. They've seen me be an old man, & now they see me be an old woman, but they don't ask silly questions about that. They are a pleasure to be with.

As are their brothers, to my never-ending surprise. The boys' rivalry has spurred them into becoming exceptional athletes & scholars. I find them interesting to talk to, as long as I'm alone with one at a time.

I hear that the incestuous queen has turned chaste. Sleeping alone, as she should have done since the day she was widowed. But if she had, her 2 lovable daughters would not be in life, delighting me & my serpents.

So much so, that I feel my dry old seer's heart become vulnerable again to hope, & thereby to fear, as I wonder what The Gods have in mind for my 2 little flowers. In my dreams I take them away with me to a land that knows no fate.

It's blasphemy, of course, which may imperil them further. I feel that I've been contaminated by the queen's obsessive worrying, with which I have little patience.

CHAPTER 23

M y women are growing noticeably older, more sedate in their applause of my rulership, more elaborate in their make-up. Which may explain Oe's continued fidelity to me.

Of course time has not stood still for me either. Yet I defy anyone who hasn't known me since childhood, to guess that I've passed the half-hundred mark, & am headed for serious old age. Madame Tiresias was quite right, on that long-ago night   when my first husband reenforced the fate he wanted to avoid   when she said that: Chastity preserved a youthful figure & complexion. The last 12 years since I stopped sharing my couch, have left few inscriptions on my face. They have not doubled my chin, nor slowed my step. Although they have drawn deep vertical lines down Oe's cheeks, & horizontal ones across his forehead. He looks much older than 33. No trace is left of the exciting boy-man who liberated our City from the Sphinx. We've grown much closer in age as we've grown less intimate. To look at us side by side, no one would imagine that we might be mother & son. But then, his chastity is not by choice, except for his surprising choice to remain faithful to me. Our marriage has settled into a typical family relationship. We might as well be a youthful mother & her prematurely aging bachelor son. We have little to say to each other when we're alone. Which both of us avoid. When we are, we play word games. We're both good at them.

At the beginning of his banishment from my couch, while I was pregnant with Ismene, I was convinced that he would seek consolation with any one of my women, given the emphasis he placed on sex in his relationship with me. I thought for sure Neirete would finally net him, with her Egyptian wiles. She is   or used to be   the most striking. & the most submissive, at least outwardly. Untiringly eager to run his errands into the mudpuddles of our City. But he has resisted all enticement, almost as though to defy me. Or Mother Nature. Unless he has been finding secret consolations during his disguised forays into the City. Perhaps he has developed a penchant for women of the people, who treat their men like baby tyrants. Or for prostitutes, of whom he feels free to ask services he   erroneously   thinks would be unacceptable inside the palace walls. Or perhaps he came into his father's sexual inheritance, the afternoon he cured me of desire for him, when he suddenly sounded & looked like his father. Perhaps he sneaks into town once a week to pick up boys. At any rate, he has made no attempt to come back to my couch since the night of the whip.

When Neirete asked to speak to me in private, last week, I had a moment of fear: that she had something unpleasant to tell me about Oe. Something I'd have to pretend to know, & explain away. I wasn't expecting her request to leave my services & return to Egypt. Her brother's wife died unexpectedly; he's asking her to supervise his household. As a replacement she offered me her oldest niece, also named Neirete, who is 17, intelligent, & most eager to serve me.

Is the niece as beautiful & accomplished as her aunt?

The accomplished aunt blushes professionally. If I think that she used to be beautiful, I will think that her niece is beautiful, too. Only more so. Her niece looks like a daughter of Aphrodite. Her hair is the color of polished copper.

I don't ask: How she knows that? Has she seen her niece lately? Neirete is one of my favorite women. She has excellent taste. & insights I can't expect from a 17-year-old, whose youth will accentuate my age. I have the fleeting foreboding that I shall rue this replacement, but I have no rational grounds to refuse it. & so I accept, telling Neirete that I shall miss her.

Then I hear that the niece has already arrived in Thebes, & has been staying in her aunt's rooms, awaiting my decision, & the moment to be presented to me & the court.

What if I had refused?

In that case, the niece would have traveled back to Egypt with her aunt.

I agree to receive the second Neirete early in the afternoon. She walks in behind her aunt, taller than her aunt, with just the right combination of shyness & defiance. She is an undeniable beauty. Noticed even by Oe, whose eyes light up for the first time in 12 years. At least in my presence. I decide that she uses henna on her long wavy hair, & ponder my premonition.

Her aunt is already dressed for travel. She looks chic, worldly. I'm sorry to see her go. After the audience I walk her to her escort. The same escort that brought the niece. Who's standing beside me, taller also than I.

CHAPTER 24

The peasants started the harvest at sunrise this morning. It promises to be the most plentiful Thebes has reaped, due to irrigation ditches Oe had them dig through the fields last spring.

This year we'll be able to export grain, instead of importing it: he's telling our treasurer. Who beams at him with such adoration, I fleetingly wonder if they're lovers. If that explains the fixed tautness in Oe's face. But he's listening to the faint rumbling I also begin to hear coming towards us, culminating in a deafening thunderclap. Followed by heavy pelting of hailstones.

Oe rushes from the throne room, to recruit every able-bodied man & woman in the palace to help the peasants bring in the crops. Several of my women rush out after him, the niece Neirete among them.

Creon & I look at each other, shaking our heads. Oe is making a mistake: my brother says: He'll lose the peasants' respect, working alongside them with his royal hands. They'll see his help as interference, & feel criticized. Besides, it's useless anyway, & they know it. The hail must have flattened every remaining stalk by now, & knocked out the grains. They're harvesting wet straw. What's left of grains will ferment, & rot.

Maybe Oe will find a way to make liquor out of the fermenting grain: I half-joke.

My brother laughs: He just might. —I don't have much luck with my husbands, do I? The first one was an

egomaniacal hypochondriac, & the second one is a mania-
cal humanitarian. It's odd, despite the diametrical differences of their goals, there's a lot of similarity between the
two.

I stare at him. Is he subtly telling me that he knows
who Oe really is. He's staring back at me. Suddenly I see
desire in his eyes. I look away.

He's sorry he foisted this juvenile hero upon me: he
says. Obviously I've grown disenchanted with him, after
an initial flurry of enthusiasm about a youthful lover. It's
amazing how fast that boyish face has aged. Those lines
down his cheeks. Real maniac lines. Laius had them, too.
Too bad we're brother & sister. & not living in Egypt.
We'd make a much better royal couple, he & I.

In the evening, the skies are serene again, with an
innocent slice of moon grinning down on the wasted
fields. We're gloomy company at dinner. Oe praises the
girls, whose hands are raw from breaking off stalks. He
praises the twins, who cut & baled like demons. He praises
our treasurer, who hurt his clerical back. He praises my
dishevelled women. But their combined efforts saved very
little, hampered as they were by the uncooperative sullen-
ness of the peasants, men & women alike. The peasants feel
that he interfered with nature, with his irrigation system. It
provoked the gods, & they were showing him what they
could do, & sent the hailstorm.

Maybe we can barter our luxury items for staples,
then we wouldn't have to deplete the just refilled treasury.
He wishes he knew of a way to dry the stuff. At least to
feed the cattle.

He should get a dragon to breathe on it: my father
Menoeceus cuts in: Dragon breath is made of wind &
sunshine. Those crops will dry in no time.

My father should get us a dragon then: Oe says in a tone of exasperation: This is not the time for hero tales.

I expect an invitation to a fight, but my father has sunk back into his peaceful stupor.

Oe's face is white & drawn. I feel sorry for him.

He shouldn't take the peasant's attitude so personally: I say to him: They're a superstitious lot. Always looking for a scapegoat when something goes wrong.

But what if they're right! Maybe the gods *are* angered by human inventiveness. One of us should go to Delphi, & find out.

He's looking from me to Creon, & back to me. He'd go himself but he doesn't want to give the impression that he's backing out. Besides, he needs to think up some use for those fermenting grains.

Creon says that: He hasn't much faith in oracles. They're usually ambiguous, & get you into deeper trouble, as you try to prevent the bad ones from coming true.

Again I wonder if he knows. After all, he was present when Laius & Chrysippus came back with their murder message. When I thought of confronting the Pythoness with the wrath of my grief. Before I knew that she was Tiresias' daughter Manto. Whom I have no desire to consult. I'm tired of entering into one-sided dialogues with invisible authorities.

Too many questions beget unwanted answers: I say: We've had hailstorms before.

What if the peasants act up?

Then we'll have to put them down: my brother says: That, too, has happened before. Nothing is new under the sun. Everything is repetition, with slight variations. Like waves cresting on the shore.

Oe hears the reference to cresting waves as a swipe at his name, as perhaps it was. He's had enough hostility in one day: he declares sullenly: He's going to sleep.

The rest of us finish our meal, then we, too, drag ourselves off to our respective quarters.

I lie awake on my couch, wondering if the hailstorm is the opening scene of the last act in this farce the gods started playing with us 34 years ago. Again I feel the bottomless grief I felt looking one last time into my name-less son's baby face, pink & blunt with sleep, as he is lifted from his bed by hands intent on murder. I felt a similar hopelessness, looking at the drawn face of the grown man at dinner. The hopelessness of a situation does not dimin-ish our responsibility to change it: I think: We must stand united against the gods. Who may yet amend their script, swayed by the truth & strength of our love. My heart floods with long-forgotten tenderness for this hopelessly struggling man. I imagine that he, too, is lying awake, torturing his brain about the crops.

Quietly I get up, & glide to his rooms. He's lying in the arms of the niece Neirete. Who notices me first, & nudges him repeatedly before he looks up. His eyes are like holes in Hades. The niece hides her face in her hennaed hair.

I excuse myself. Then ask the niece if she feels un-comfortable in her aunt's old rooms, now that her aunt is gone. Would she like me to arrange for different accom-modations for her?

She shakes her face clear of her mane, & slides off Oe's couch, standing across from me, tall, in naked splen-dor. Thanking me for my   unnecessary   kindness. She's comfortable right where she is.

Such impudence calls for the whip. Oe's charioteer whip is hanging on the wall beside me, tempting my hand. I use a smile instead, & words. Congratulations! I say: May she remain welcome right where she is.

Then I quickly state my reason for interrupting their coitus. I'd come to suggest that we send our treasurer to Delphi, if Oe still feels that we need oracular advice to solve our harvest problem. & retrieve my steps

Good night, Queen Jocasta! the niece calls after me.

Back on my couch, I don't know if I should laugh or cry. I opt for laughing.

CHAPTER 25

The treasurer returned from Delphi with the cryptic message that: All will be well in Thebes if we get rid of a descendant of the sown man.

My father Menoeceus hears the words: SOWN MAN & instantly teeters to his gouty feet. He calls for his armor. It still fits him, except for the leg & foot protections. Never mind: he says: he'll be a warrior in houseshoes.

He orders a long ladder to be placed against the north wall, & has 4 sturdy men hoist him up the rungs. We watch him weave on top of the wall, swaying precariously. Several times it looks as though he's about to fall back into the city, but finally he leans forward, & plunges to his death outside.

Oe dismisses my father's self-sacrifice as an empty act of bravado. He seized upon a pretext to play the hero one last time. He was tired of being an old man.

But Creon & I admire his unquestioning devotion. We should all die so courageously. & he impressed our citizens, who trust the wisdom of their ancient founder. He still had glamor for them, even if he looked like a puzzled turtle most of the time. A decaying dragon's tooth. They're appeased. Confident that all will be well now. The peasants stop filling in Oe's irrigation ditches.

But all is *not* well. Rough hands shake me awake in the middle of the night. I bolt up into Oe's distorted face bending over me, & my instinct tells me that something has gone wrong with the niece Neirete. Who may be pregnant. &/or tired of his sexual persistence, sooner than I grew tired of it. & that he's blaming me for it.

But what he has come to tell me is much worse. The niece Neirete is running a high fever. Blue & green boils are erupting on her beautiful face & body. Oe is sure that she has the plague. He thinks her mother probably died of it in Egypt. Her poor lovely daughter will die of it in Thebes. He's keeping her hidden in his apartments. No one must find out about it, or the people will panic. He needs my help to keep the secret. I must tell my women at the morning audience   —who will tell all of Thebes—

that I sent Neirete back to Egypt because I surprised her in my husband's arms.

I agree that the girl's illness must remain unnoticed. But I refuse to project a cliché of the jealous wife to my women. I will tell them that I allowed the niece Neirete to go back to Egypt because she was homesick.

Which they're less likely to believe: Oe interjects with a sneer.

They'll pretend to believe it, & imagine the other reason. The girl probably has been flaunting her conquest to them anyhow. So soon, in less than a month after her arrival. She succeeded where all the others failed.

But under no circumstances must he continue to keep her on his couch! Doesn't he realize how contagious she is! He should smuggle her out of the sleeping palace right now, & take her to the building Laius set up for the sick outside the city walls. I'll help him, if he wants me to. We'll put heavy veils over her face, & walk her out between us. & if anybody sees us, we'll say that she's going back to Egypt, & order an escort.

No way! He's not about to abandon the beautiful, sweet woman who gave his manhood back to him. After I castrated him 12 years ago. For 12 years he has lived like a eunuch beside me, & the first time he reaches out again, his love is condemned to death. His voice breaks; he clears his throat.

Neirete thinks that I have evil powers. That I put a curse on her for finding her with him. & for how she spoke to me. He doesn't believe that. I don't care enough about him to do evil. & with my religious hang-ups, I'd be too afraid of the gods.

I didn't castrate him! I protest: I merely asked for a respite from constant sex & pregnancies.

& I didn't begrudge him Neirete either. Although I found her insolence quite uncalled for. Perhaps her illness is her punishment for that insolence. But it is not of my doing! I believe that we get back what we give out. It is that belief rather than fear of the gods that keeps me from casting evil spells. —If I have the power to cast them.

My women will believe that I cast such a spell, if they find out that Neirete lies dying in Hades Hall.

What if they find out that she's dying   of the plague   on his couch. Right here near them in the palace? They'll be hysterical. They might even think he gave it to her. Believing that it is sexually transmitted, & that he is a carrier, who gives it to others, but never gets it himself. They'll think that I found out 12 years ago, when I stopped sleeping with him.

Let them think what they want. He can't worry about that now. He came to warn me, now it's up to me to feed them hypocrisies. He needs to go back to the poor sweet woman. Who will die on his couch, no matter what I tell him. He will stay beside her, & hold her hot wet hands. He'll do what he can to give her comfort, for as long as it takes. That's the least he can do for her.

.   .   .

An hour later he is back. Neirete has died. He could use my help, disposing of her body. If I'm still willing to help. Mercifully it's still dark.

A gagging odor fills the room where Neirete lies, unrecognizable. In silence we dress her in a long travel tunic. We shroud her disfigured face in heavy veils. Between us, we walk her out of the palace. We meet no one.

It's a long walk to Hades Hall, but we're afraid to wake the stable crew, if we take a chariot, or a horse.

The guard at the gate is asleep. We tiptoe past. As soon as we're beyond the range of his torch, Oe slings the body over his shoulder. It speeds our pace.

That gate was already badly guarded the first time he walked through it: Oe says. He wonders if it could still be the same man. It seems a lifetime ago.

Then he wonders about our risk of catching Neirete's disease.

None: I say: I don't believe that dying of an illness is the punishment the gods have in mind for us.

Punishment? What have we done that deserves divine punishment? Except for having loved badly. For which he blames himself. He was addicted to sleeping with me; it killed my love for him. Even his mother wrote him that a woman needed to recover the privacy of her body, after childbirth.

Yes: I say: She wrote that to me, too.

Rats escape as we pry open the stone trough behind Laius' building. Oe tenderly lays Neirete down inside it, on her back, looking at the stars. He pours fragrant oil over her body, & sets it aflame.

It takes a long time to burn a human being. Especially one as tall & filled out as Neirete. It makes a lot of smoke, & it smells bad, despite the strong scent of the oil.

When we replace the slab on the trough, the night is changing into a pale blue morning. In silence we walk back toward our city. I take his hand. Which presses mine. 12 years of hard feelings have gone up in Neirete's smelly smoke.

As we pass the fork in the road, at the rock where the Sphinx used to crouch, we hear footsteps at a distance behind us. We turn, & see a tall woman with flowing hair walking rapidly toward us. Silhouetted against the rising sun, her hair glows red.

We stand aghast, sure that we're seeing Neirete. But as she comes closer, she becomes a stranger. A messenger Tiresias' daughter Manto is sending, to clarify her previous oracle.

The amended version says: Expel the murderer of King Laius.

The murderer? Oedipus looks puzzled: Hadn't King Laius died in a chariot accident?

That's what we'd always assumed: I say: How odd.

I tell the messenger who we are, but she already knew, or she wouldn't have given us the message. She's a seer also.

She declines my invitation to walk to Thebes with us the rest of the way, & relax in the palace for a few days. She bids us goodbye, & hurries back on the road to Delphi. Oedipus admires her stamina, but I think that she may know also who we are to each other. Perhaps she even knows that we just secretly burned & buried a young Egyptian woman, the first person to die of the plague in our city.

I try to persuade Oedipus to keep the amended oracle to ourselves. Why publicize it? The people are appeased with my father's sacrifice. What good will a witch hunt do to find the perpetrator of a murder committed 17 years ago?

But he's determined to track down whoever killed his predecessor. He'll conduct a thorough investigation. He'll interogate Laius' old charioteers. The former health spies. He'll put up an award. We must do what the gods are telling us to do, before the plague claims any more victims. If only he knew of a cure.

I don't object that: a successful investigation will lead to his own indictment. I'm tired of trying to protect him from his fate. Of pitting my intelligence against the games of the gods.

As we enter the palace, we cross 2 servants carrying a basin with cold water. The treasurer has taken ill, & wishes to lower his fever. Oedipus hurries off with them.

My women react with dull stares to my announcement that I allowed the homesick Neirete to return to Egypt. After the audience, 2 of them come to me, asking for a 1-year leave from my services. They're Egyptians also. Sisters, which I didn't know, & don't believe. They need to take care of urgent family business. I don't tell them that, if they're running from the plague, they're running in the wrong direction. That it was the niece Neirete who brought the plague with her from Egypt. I wish them a safe trip.

Half an hour later I see them already outside the south gate, with one of our stable hands. Who's Egyptian also.

CHAPTER 26

Oedipus' thorough murder investigation is stirring up a lot of bitter feelings. Some of Laius' old charioteers claim that they always knew there'd been foul play behind their king's alleged accident. He'd been much too experienced a driver to let 2 shying horses throw him off, & drag him to his death. They wouldn't be at all surprised if the king's former lover had had a hand in it. They'd never understood why Chrysippus had left so abruptly, under the cover of night, 30 some years ago. Right after he & the king returned from Delphi, where they'd gone to consult the oracle about the future of the new heir to the throne. Who'd had no future; not even a name yet. Who'd died of crib death, the very night they'd come back. As the oracle must have told them he would, to judge by their returning king's somber face.

Maybe Chrysippus had come back as quietly as he had left, & ambushed their king. Once again on his way to Delphi, this time to find out how to get rid of the Sphinx. The old king sure hadn't had much luck with his trips to Delphi.

Oedipus is astounded that I had a son with Laius —who, I'd told him, preferred men on his couch—   & never mentioned it to him. When we'd been so close, during the first 2½ years of our marriage.

My little son's death left a deep wound in my heart: I say: I was afraid to reopen it, if I spoke about him. He'd only lived for 2 months. & he'd been such a healthy, intelligent baby.

Oedipus tries to comfort me. He realizes that this investigation must be reviving painful memories for me. He wishes he could spare me. But justice must be done. It's the command of the gods. What a tragedy to lose one's child. King Laius must have felt horrible, bringing me the bad news back from Delphi.

Yes, horrible.

How long ago was that?

I can see on his face that he's reassessing my age. Figuring: how many years? with furrowed brow.

Please: I say: I really don't want to talk about it.

He's sorry he upset me. He's just following up on every lead he can get, to solve this murder mystery. He's sending runners to every city in Greece, to locate Chrysippus, & invite him to Thebes, to answer the charges of the old charioteers. —Some of whom are volunteering to go looking for him themselves.

It's a waste of time & effort. Not to mention expense. Chrysippus did not kill Laius.

How can I know that?

I was there the night he left. He did not leave in anger. They had not quarrelled. Not even argued.

Why did he leave then?

I shrug. He was growing up, becoming a man. Perhaps he wished for a less dependent life: I say hesitantly. Unable to say that: Chrysippus left because he was shocked & disgusted by his lover murdering the child he had helped to create, on my couch.

In that case, isn't it conceivable that he came back to erase the memory of his dependence by killing the man who had used him sexually?

Anything is possible: I sigh: Anything but the truth.

Undeterred, Oedipus sends for the chief runner. A different man reports in his stead. The chief runner has succumbed to the plague.

That makes 88 Thebans who have died of it so far, not counting the Egyptian Neirete. We're carting the corpses out to Hades Hall, & burn them in the reopened trough in back of it. Several of the former health spies applied for the job of transporting the dead out there, in the rickety old carts they'd kept stored away all these years. It's high-risk work, which pays accordingly. Once again we see men with half-hidden faces, their mouths & noses covered with limejuice-soaked strips of cloth, standing tall on carts filled with horizontal bodies. Once again people start running when they hear them rattle down a street.

Most of them are quite old by now, but they still resent Creon & me for disbanding them, 17 years ago. Now they're coming out of their silent loathing to accuse Creon &/or me of having conspired to assassinate their old king. They say that either of us sneaked into the stables just before Laius' last departure for Delphi, & craftily loosened one of the wheels on his chariot, to cause the vehicle to tilt out of control at the first sharp turn in the road. They'd always known that Creon & I hated their king's hygienic rulership. —During which, however, no plague had occurred!

I don't ask Oedipus if he'll also invite my brother & me to answer the charges of the former health spies. He's too beaten to be confronted with logic.

CHAPTER 27

Several hours after dinner, a middle-aged midwife appears before me, looking distraught & tearful. Before I can ask how she managed to reach my rooms, unannounced & unimpeded, she tells me in Oedipus' normal voice that: The people hate him. They say: He's a madman, who's killing them with his crazy innovations. Those ditches he made them dig through the fields brought on the hailstorm that ruined the harvest. Now those foul-tasting potions he sends their wives & children have brought on a disease. The queen's second is worse than her first. Who was crazy, too, but at least he didn't provoke the gods, trying to improve on nature. & he didn't concoct stuff that make them sick.

An elderly stonecutter had bought the midwife a cup of wine, then launched into a long tirade: How he wouldn't be surprised if it was the second husband who'd widowed the queen in the first place. Hadn't he appeared in the city right after the first one had his so-called accident? Well, to his thinking, maybe the second husband ran into the first one somewhere along the road, & didn't like his looks, or his bearing, & did him in. Before he did in the old Sphinx. Maybe a murderer had been sitting on the throne of Thebes all these merry years, & no one knew it. Except the murderer, who was now conducting this hypocritical investigation, to deflect the logical suspicion from himself, after the latest oracle called for the expulsion of the first husband's murderer.

I take a deep breath, & silently admire the elderly stonecutter's logical suspicion, wondering how many of our citizens may be sharing it. A ruler should never underestimate the intelligence of the people.

The midwife smiles pitifully: I have to admit that he was right when he told me that the people don't suspect his disguise. The old stonecutter was sure he was talking to an old midwife   —whose bottom he pinched, every time he felt particularly proud of a logical absurdity. Or do I think he would have accused the king of murder to his face?

I shrug.

It's shocking what the people are saying about him. Do I think he should abdicate, & devote the rest of his life to caring for the sick? Has he been such a bad king?

I shake my head. How can I tell him that: Yes! I think that, if he abdicated, & left Thebes, Laius' murderer would technically be expelled, the oracle's requirement would be met, & the plague might cease, without also telling him that: the lecherous old stonecutter's logic is pretty accurate. & that there are even more absurdities behind the total truth. He wouldn't believe me. He's still genuinely unaware of having killed anyone, on his beggar's walk to Thebes, 17 years ago.

The twins say: He's a rotten ruler. They've been pestering him about abdicating. The sooner the better. They're in agreement, can I believe that! for the first time in the 16 years of their life. What a shame that what suddenly unites them is contempt for their father. Do I think he has been a bad father to them?

I shake my head.

They want him to get out of Thebes, & let them take over. Eteocles will rule the first year, since he was the first

one to come out of me, & Polyneices will rule the next
year. & so on in alternation.

When he objected that: They weren't old enough for
rulership, they said: He hadn't been that much older when
he took over, after he married the throne. It was only after
he grew 'old enough' that he started messing up.

His protest that: He was responsible neither for the
hailstorm nor for the plague, was met with laughter.

—In unison, can I believe that!— He must have done
something pretty wrong, or the gods wouldn't have it in
for him: they replied: Maybe the gods didn't appreciate his
meddling with nature. Maybe his always trying to know
better offended them. Or maybe he was the murderer he
was pretending to track down with his pedantic investigation. Maybe he had killed the old king to sit in his place.

The twins talked just like the peasants. Like the
stonecutter. & on top of that they were laughing at him. A
hideous chorus of ridicule, from his own sons. Whom he
hadn't the stamina to punish. He probably should have
been stricter with them when they were little, but he has
never believed in punishing children. He's always thought
they'd respond best to love. He certainly doesn't think he
deserves their disrespect.

I don't point out that my father Menoeceus didn't
deserve his grandson's disrespect either, even if the grandson didn't know that his father-in-law, the decaying dragon's
tooth, was also his grandfather.

I feel sorry for the defeated man in midwife's clothing. Once again I blame myself for having forced him into
his hopeless life. But I no longer tell myself that the
hopelessness of the situation does not relieve me from my
responsibility to improve it. I've tried too hard for too
long.

I get him an amphora of his favorite red wine & a cup. I throw a cover over the midwife's pathetic legs on his couch. I kiss the furrowed forehead, like a mother might, & tell him: Go to sleep.

CHAPTER 28

The number of plague victims has passed the 200 mark. Madame Tiresias comes to me before the morning audience, to request release from her vow of silence. The time has come to tell the king. Enough innocent people have died to keep my guilty secret.

I don't challenge her to name just one person who died on my account. I shrug. Which she can't see, & would interpret as arrogance, if she could see it. I know she doesn't like me. Especially not when she's a woman. She dislikes me, along with the female phases of her life. She knows I kept silent only in the hope of improving my son's hopeless fate.

Which   unlike mine   seems to touch her old seer's heart. Can she not foresee the consequences of her revelation? How does she think Oedipus will react to what she feels she has to tell him? Will he believe her, even? Will anyone believe her?

But that is her concern, not mine. I will be no part of it any longer. The moment she opens her mouth I shall walk from the throne room under the pretext of an overdue sacrifice. I shall bow out with dignity, the way the shining moon slips behind a cloud.

I make Madame Tiresias sit on my couch & wait, while I put on my ceremonial robes   perfume my hair fasten Oedipus' radiant sun brooch on my right shoulder the silver moon brooch on the left   my brother's dragon clasp around my left arm. When I have finished, the silver

panel obligingly reflects a regal highpriestess, ready to meet
the gods.

I overcome the slight revulsion I always feel for
Tiresias, whether male or female, & take her elbow to steer
her down the hall. She stiffens, equally repulsed by my
touch.

Go ahead: I say to her: Tell him if you must.

But the time to tell has not yet come. A special
messenger has arrived from Corinth. King Polybus has
died   in his sleep; with a smile on his face. Queen
Periboea wants Oedipus to come back & take the vacant
seat on the throne. Could he not be a king to both cities?
Divide the year between 2 worlds, like the godly daughter
Core, & rule 3 months over Corinth, & 9 over Thebes, or
the other way round?

I study Oedipus' intense face, & see relief replace
grief for the man he thinks was his father. Whom he loved,
& lived in the fear of killing, as the oracle had told him he
would. Who has now relieved him of that 17-year-long
fear by dying of his own accord. Must that not also relieve
him of his dread of bedding down with the by-now-
ancient Queen Periboea?

I urge him to fulfill the Queen's request. She is bereft,
& very old. He should go to her at once.

But what about the murder investigation?

It can be continued during his absence.

Of course. He didn't mean to imply that he's irre-
placeable.

Creon smiles a thin-lipped smile in my direction. He
has been staring at my ceremonial dress. I wish I could
spare him the grief I am about to cause him.

Madame Tiresias is fidgeting, clearing her throat.

The special messenger hands Oedipus a letter from
Queen Periboea. A long letter, in her minute, convoluted

writing. Which he begs Oedipus not to read until he has
heard what else he has to say. Which   he must think
are glad tidings, to judge by his radiant face. His eyes are
clear & brilliant, like fountain water in sunlight.

He is an old shepherd, possibly in his sixties, with the
landscape-like beauty nature sometimes bestows on those
living close to her. He looks like a noble ram, with grey
curls in the place of horns.

Queen Periboea chose him to bring the news, because he has a special relationship to King Oedipus: he
begins slowly, as though about to tell a story around a fire
in the pastures at night: He is, you might say, a kind of
midwife to the king.

I hear a smile behind his voice, & know the story.
A story that would have fulfilled my most desperate wish,
had I heard it 35 years ago. Yet, I want to hear it even
now. I'll finally know how my little son was saved.

—For his doom.— & I shall reward the savior. Who
expects to be rewarded. Not out of greed, but out of joy in
his good deed. A joy in which he expects us all to share at
the end of his story.

He starts telling us how it all happened: On a clear fall
night, filled with shooting stars. He'd still been young
then. His first summer out alone with the herd. Which he
was getting ready to drive back to Corinth.

Suddenly old Picus is standing before him. Picus the
Woodpecker, a shepherd from Thebes who'd been graz-
ing his flocks alongside him all summer. He's breathless, &
in a panic. He's too old to be running like that. He can
barely speak. He hands him a bundle, wrapped in a blanket, which he asks him to take away with him to Corinth.

The blanket is of the finest quality. He can tell, he
knows wool. & inside is a little boy, also of the finest
quality. Whom a powerful Theban has ordered old Picus

to put to death. But old Picus can't do it. He's a shepherd. He recognizes good livestock when he sees it. & he figures: As long as the child is out of Thebes, it's like dead to the powerful man who lives there.

The then-still-young shepherd takes the little boy in the blanket, & carries him all the way to Corinth. Making him drink ewes' milk directly from the teat.

While they walk, he's thinking: The king & queen of Corinth have no children... The palace would be a good home for a well-born little boy from Thebes...

Whom the king & queen want to adopt as soon as they see him, rosy-cheeked, with alert little eyes. But the news of a royal adoption might travel to Thebes, & put the child in danger. Not to mention old Picus. They decide that Queen Periboea will pretend to give birth to the little boy. Surrounded by her women she walks to the seashore, with the child hidden under her tunic, making her look very pregnant. She squats down, cries out in pain for a while, then pulls him from between her legs. They name him the child of the Cresting Wave.

But now that King Polybus has died, & the man who ordered the baby killed probably also died, or is at least peacefully old, the Queen feels that Oedipus needs to know where he came from. & that he's welcome back in Corinth nonetheless.

The relief I saw on Oedipus' face at the news of King Polybus' natural death has changed back to anguish. That old shepherd   Picus   is he still alive? he asks.

No. He died abruptly, some 15 maybe 18 years ago. His son took over for him.

My brother Creon remembers Picus. He was one of King Laius' most trusted shepherds. & so devoted to the king, he hanged himself a month or so after the king died.

Oedipus looks at him: Could that old shepherd be the

murderer we're looking for?

Creon protests: Absolutely not!

The messenger's radiance turns to shock.

Madame Tiresias clears her throat again.

I rise. I walk over to the the beautiful old man & give him the moon brooch from my left shoulder. He did a noble deed: I say: & old Picus acted nobly, too. More nobly than many a wellborn person might have acted in the situation.

I look around the room, & excuse myself to all assembled: I need to offer a long-due scrifice.

I feel a hundred eyes boring into my back on my way out.

I'm passing through the East Gate, when I hear a roar behind me. Perhaps not a roar so much, as a bellow. Boundless pain, condensed into sound. Oedipus' reply to Madame Tiresias' revelation. It whips me forward to the rock on which the Sphinx crouched, 17 years ago.

An inaccessible rock, to a woman without wings. But there are cracks in the stone, where the wingless woman can fit her toes. My father Menoeceus jumped to his sacrificial death, a warrior in houseshoes. I shall jump to mine, a barefoot queen, a highpriestess of Hera, with a drop of dragon blood boiling in my veins.

My knees & hands are bloody when I reach the top. My ceremonial robe tears along the left side as I go into a crouch. I apologize for my imperfections to the immortal intelligence of the Sphinx, whom I invoke to propel my leap. After all, we were defeated by the same man.

EPILOGUE

O Walrus, Old Walrus, my last friend in this world of enemies. I'm writing to you from the bottom of the deepest pit. Did I really ride so high, to have fallen this far down into damnation? My rulership is over. My sons are hounding me to abdicate, united suddenly in contempt for their father. Who is also their brother, as we all found out today.

I'm getting out of this plague-infested city   —which was my city after all; always has been—   & become a beggar once again. An old beggar, this time, a defeated old man, whose removal will magically restore my people's health. Such is the promise of the gods, who never smiled on me. Who only pretended to smile on the treasures I heaped upon their altars, in ignorantly grateful sacrifice. They had damned me from birth, but I didn't know it until today. Now I must walk the roads of Greece in expiation for horrors I didn't know I was committing.

Remember the arrogant charioteer I wrote to you about, who wouldn't let me pass, on the narrow road from Delphi to Thebes? Who threatened me with his whip, because I looked like a beggar. A young beggar, who had just been chastened by the abominable oracle I also wrote to you about, in that same first report from here, & asked you never to repeat to anybody. Which I thought I had escaped by staying away from Corinth, in my ignorance. It has all come true, Walrus! Not only did the arrogant charioteer die in his fight with me   or mine with him   he

was also the former King of Thebes, my predecessor Laius.
& not only that: He was my father! I am the murderer I
was tracking down with my conscientious investigation. I
am the parricide the oracle was cursing. Now who do you
think my mother is!!!!!

Yes, Walrus, you were quite right to call me a bastard. &
ultimately it was because of your constant taunting that I
fell into this pit. That unknown father of mine, King Laius
of Thebes, my eventual murder victim, also consulted the
oracle, & was told the same thing I was told 18 years later.
& just like me, he wanted to make sure it wouldn't come
true. But unlike me, he was brutal about it. He didn't
renounce anything, or deprive himself in any way. He
simply handed the baby I was to an old shepherd of his, to
do away with me. I don't know if my mother protested. If
she knew about it even. All I know is that she mourned me
for 18 years. She was still in mourning   —for me; not
for her husband—   the first time I saw her. Saw her
consciously, I mean, even if I didn't know she was mourning me. I didn't even know she'd had a child with Laius
until I started the murder investigation. The old shepherd
had a nobler heart than my royal father. He disobeyed   at
great risk to his life; so great a risk, he committed suicide
when I returned to Thebes, even though my father, his
king, was dead by then. He handed me over to a shepherd
from Corinth. Who handed me over to his king & queen.
...You know the rest...

Having killed an arrogant unknown, who had ordered me
to be killed   his own son! & only a baby   so that I
wouldn't grow up to kill him, isn't what troubles me the
most. He must have been a very selfish man. Maybe I
would have killed him even if I had known him as my
father. All the more, maybe. After all, I was following
divine instructions. What troubles me   abjectly   is my

relationship with Jocasta. I'm ashamed to look her in the face, just to bid her goodbye.

I now think that she must have found out somehow who she & I had been to each other before. Before we married, I mean. Maybe Tiresias told her then what he told me today, & she stopped being intimate with me from that day on. Remember what I wrote to you about her saying that: she had a 'mother body' which needed the couch all to itself, when she got pregnant with our youngest child, Ismene. If only she had told me. It totally destroyed me, remember? I couldn't understand what I'd done to her all of a sudden. Why she seemed to cringe at my touch, after 2½ years of such passion. Requited passion! The memory of it makes me

Dear Sir,

I continue the letter my father is unable to finish himself, having just injured his eyes with one of my mother's shoulder brooches. He is in terrible pain. He says he'd hoped that hurting his body would diminish the agony in his heart over the suicide of my mother. Who was his mother also, which we all found out today. & which is why she drowned herself in the sea, at the same spot the Sphinx drowned herself before I was born. One of my mother's attendants just found her sandals at the foot of the Sphinx's rock, & brought them to my father while he was writing to you.

So many horrible things are happening today. I cannot quite feel everything just yet. Please don't think that I'm callous, not weeping for my mother at this time. I will when I can think more clearly. At least she has stopped her pain. It's my father who needs all of me now.

My Uncle Creon   to whom my mother was the most important other person in the world   is banishing him from our city, because the oracle demands it in order for the plague to cease. My uncle says: No punishment is harsh enough for the man who drove his sister to her death. I don't think my father ever drove my mother to do anything. She was a very independent woman. I don't understand why he needs to be expelled for killing my grandfather either. Even if we now find out that my maternal grandfather was the same as my paternal grandfather. That my father's father was also his father-in-law. It all sounds horribly complicated. & my father didn't know anything about it. He just lived. & he cared deeply for every one of us. He helped many people, but now everyone is turning against him. Even my brothers.

You cannot imagine an unhappier man. He says he'll wander the roads of Greece as a beggar, & I shall go with him. He needs someone to guide his steps, because he made himself blind with my mother's brooch. Perhaps that will make him into a seer, like our dear old Tiresias who is blind also. Perhaps now father will no longer do reprehensible things he doesn't know are reprehensible.

I will try to steer him to Corinth, where Queen Periboea
    who used to be my grandmother   will perhaps not close her house to him. She wrote that she wanted him to come back & help her rule over Corinth. Where I hope you are still his friend. He has no friends left in Thebes. People now think it's bad luck to touch him, or even to speak to him.

Respectfully,
Antigone
(I am his oldest daughter...his oldest sister)

II

Dear Sister,

Our poor father died 4 days ago in Colonus, in Attica. I had left him seated in a shady grove, while I went in search of food. I found myself unexpectedly welcomed by Theseus, the king of Athens, who had heard of father's tragic fate, & greatly respected him as a ruler. He calls him: A horribly maligned model for modern kings.

Theseus returned to the grove with me, bearing a delicate meal, & wine. But father could no longer eat or drink. We think he died of a heart attack. He was clasping his throat with both hands. I grieve for him deeply. For his life more than for his death. He longed to die. Mostly, I think, because of mother's suicide, which he felt he had caused. He spoke about her incessantly   obsessively   while we wandered aimlessly about. I tried to steer us toward Corinth, but he was ashamed to go where people knew him. His shame hounded him every step of the way, no matter what I came up with to argue it away. He'd almost agree with me, but then he'd blame himself again. How can you blame yourself for loving?

It gives me deep satisfaction that Theseus buried his body with the highest honors, in Athens, in the Precinct of the Solemn Ones. Please tell all who need to know. Especially about the honorable burial. It might revise their opinion of father. Nobody in Thebes seems to understand how good he was, except perhaps Tiresias. Eteocles & Polyneices mistake his caring involvement with people for weakness. & Uncle Creon thinks nobody was good enough for mother, except he himself. At least that is how it seems to me.

Father was so worried that holding my hand might be misinterpreted, we finally acquired a staff, & both held on to it. The time I spent with him taught me one thing: There's safety at the bottom of the pit. That may be what mother sought in drowning. Now father has found it, too. I expect to be home within a month, my travels speeded courtesy of Theseus.

My love to you, & to Tiresias' serpents. Scratch their inquisitive heads for me.

ANT

III

As soon as Antigone leads her blinded father/brother through the North Gate, the city heals itself behind them. People infected with the plague get well over night. Within a month, the boy-king Eteocles restores the prosperity lost in the hailstorm. The citizens worship him.

However, with Oedipus gone, the twins are deprived of the unifying focus for their hatred. They instantly revert to their life-long rivalry. Wherever possible, Polyneices tries to stir up rebellion against his brother, & sabotage the reconstruction program.

At the end of the year, when Polyneices' turn comes to assume rulership, the citizens petition Eteocles to remain their king. Creon seconds their request, & Eteocles complies. Outraged, Polyneices raises outside forces, & lays siege to Thebes.

After much bloodshed on both sides, the enemy twins agree to settle the succession once & for all in single combat. They had rehearsed for it since birth, as tiny

warriors straining toward each other with furiously raised
baby fists. & even before that, battling in their mother's
womb. Both are champion fighters. They kill each other
in a last spectacular combat.

Once again, Creon The Ruler steps into the fore-
ground. To discourage future rebellion he decrees that
Eteocles, the lawful brother, will be buried with the highest honors, while the rebel twin's body will be left to rot,
a prey to birds & roaming dogs.

Antigone, the ever-caring little mother, disobeys &
buries Polyneices during the night. When Creon finds out,
he reluctantly sentences her to be buried alive in the very
tomb she dug for Polyneices, in order to set an example for
other potential rebels.

Tiresias, who had little sympathy for Jocasta, but
dotes on her daughters, entreats Creon to set Antigone
free. Warning that his own house will perish & all of
Thebes with it, if he lets her die.

By the time Creon believes the old seer, & runs to
reopen the tomb, it is too late. He finds Antigone dead,
with his son lying beside her, dead in her arms. Some say
that he found Ismene also, who had insisted on dying with
her sister, & that his son was lying dead between them.
Whereupon he kills himself for grief, & is buried with
them.

After that, Thebes deteriorates. An Athenian army
lays siege to the city, sent by Theseus to avenge Antigone.
The remaining citizens sneak out during the night. Among
them 175-year-old Tiresias, now once again a man. At
their first rest stop he bends down to drink from a spring,
& falls dead into the water.

Dramatis Personæ

ANTIGONE   Little Mother, oldest daughter of JOCASTA & OEDIPUS.

APOLLO   God of prophecy & healing.

ATHENA   Goddess known for chastity & martial arts.

BOETIA   The Heiferland, where Thebes was built.

CADMUS   From the East, founder of Thebes.

CHRYSIPPUS   Golden Horse, lover of LAIUS.

CORE   Maiden, daughter of the earth goddess DEMETER; she spends 9 months of the year in the Underworld.

CREON   The Ruler, brother of JOCASTA.

ERINNY   Fury, female avenging spirit.

ETEOCLES   True Glory, son of JOCASTA & OEDIPUS.

HAEMON   Bloody, son of CREON—either devoured by the Sphinx or lover of ANTIGONE.

HEPHAESTUS   He Who Shines By Day, god known for his ugliness, reputed goldsmith.

HERA   Protectress—of marriage, top goddess, wife & sister of ZEUS.

ISMENE   Knowledgeable, youngest daughter of JOCASTA & OEDIPUS.

JOCASTA	The Shining Moon, Queen of Thebes, wife of LAIUS, mother & wife of OEDIPUS.
LAIUS	Owner of Cattle, King of Thebes, husband of JOCASTA, father of OEDIPUS.
MANTO	Prophetess, a pythoness of DELPHI, daughter of TIRESIAS.
MENOECEUS	Strength of the House, father of Jocasta & Creon, a 'Sown Man', sprung from a dragon's tooth, a founder of Thebes.
MOPSUS	(Calf?), a noted seer, son of MANTO, grandson of TIRESIAS.
NEIRETE	A woman from Egypt, also the woman's niece.
OEDIPUS	Of the Cresting Wave, son of JOCASTA & LAIUS, husband of JOCASTA; King of Thebes.
PERIBOEA	Surrounded by Cattle, Queen of Corinth, adoptive mother of OEDIPUS.
POLYBUS	Much Cattle, King of Corinth, adoptive father of OEDIPUS.
POLYNEICES	Much Strife, son of JOCASTA & OEDIPUS.
PROMETHEUS	Forethought, a martyr, perpetually punished for introducing the use of fire to mortals.
PYTHONESS	An elderly virgin who sits on a tripod amidst sulphur fumes, & delivers oracles at Delphi.
SPHINX	A fable figure, composed of a bull's chest, lion's paws & tail, eagle's wings, & a human (female?) head, said to symbolize the 4 fixed signs of the Zodiac (Taurus/Leo/Scorpio/Aquarius).
THESEUS	He Who Lays Down, King of Athens.
ZEUS	Bright Sky, Top God, Father of The Heavens, husband & brother of HERA.